I0464639

The Power
of
Ethics

The Thoughtful Leader's Model for
Sustainable Competitive Advantage

With special sections on building an ethical organization in a
hostile environment, the Ethics Hall of Fame, and real-world
case studies.

Pete Geissler and Bill O'Rourke

Copyright © The Expressive Press, 2014. All rights reserved. No part of this book may be reproduced or transmitted in any form or by any means, electronic or mechanical, including photocopying, recording, or by any information storage and retrieval system, without permission in writing from the publisher.

Second Edition, 2014
The Expressive Press
www.TheExpressivePress.com

ISBN-13: 978-1511834353

ISBN-10: 1511834358

Books from Pete Geissler
- The Power of Writing Well
- The Power of Being Articulate
- The Power of Dignity
- Divorce can be Such Sweet Sorrow
- Bigshots' Bull$^{*!@\#}$

Books from The Expressive Press
- VB.Net Web Development by Dr. Charles Wood
- The Little Black Book of Human Resources Management by Barry Wolfe

The Power of Ethics
Pete Geissler. and Bill O'Rourke

UNIVERSAL PRAISE FOR THE POWER OF ETHICS

"Pete Geissler and Bill O'Rourke have written a book that elevates the subject of ethics to its rightful place: to the forefront of our thoughts and actions. The authors, sure to be early inductees into the Ethics Hall of Fame, relate rock-solid anecdotes of ethical and unethical behavior that resonate. Written in everyday prose that avoids academic murkiness, I recommend this book to a wide spectrum of readers who seek confirmation and encouragement for continued ethical behavior in their everyday work lives and beyond."

- Don Nusser, Vice President, major international consulting firm.

"This book provides a valuable addition to the ethics discussion in plain language that will appeal to a broad audience of readers. Pete and Bill effectively use their collective experience to highlight the need for and benefits of ethical behavior and the ease with which people at all levels of organizations can slip into incrementally greater levels of unethical behavior. I teach a senior Leader-ship Seminar based on virtuous leadership and the ethical challenges of leadership, which can be many, and I clearly see the need for more writing and further illumination of the importance of ethical behavior. "

- Daniel K. Donnelly, Ph.D., Dean, School of Business, Aquinas College, Nashville, Tennessee

"My heartiest thanks to you for contributing so much to our students' learning, and to increasing their sensitivity to ethical issues. You, your presentations, and your book make a big difference! Bill, I thoroughly enjoy hearing you speak, and so do my students. I received overwhelmingly positive comments from my colleagues as well."

- Jeff Thompson, Ph.D. Associate Professor, Romney Institute of Public Management, Brigham Young University, Provo, Utah

"Organizations and individuals that behave ethically enjoy a commanding and enduring lead in achieving success in business and enjoying true happiness in life; I've witnessed that phenomenon-non so many times during my 35-plus years in business that I consider it conventional wisdom. Now readers of this book can witness the same through the eyes and minds of the authors, two keen observers of business and academe and practicing ethicists. Enjoy and profit."

- Paul Spence, Vice President, Highmark, Inc., Pittsburgh, Pennsylvania.

4

"I am delighted to endorse The Power of Ethics as a very practical application of real-world experience where ethics meets the business world. I worked for Bill O'Rourke when he was President of Alcoa Russia and I know that his ethics had a profound impact on the organization and on me. I heartily recommend this resource for you to learn from Bill's wisdom and example, as I have. This is not a recitation of academic studies-- Bill and Pete walk the talk and encourage the rest of us to live up to their example."

- Bryan G. Eagle, Managing Partner, Eagle Consultancy International, Pittsburgh PA and Moscow

"This book should be mandatory reading--no, studying and absorbing--for every corporate officer and employee of any business! Understanding the correlation between ethics and moral beliefs is vital to a successful business.

"Rationalizing unjust and corrupt business practices goes beyond the penalties of those found guilty. The ramifications of unethical behavior will compromise businesses for generations to come. Learn why being ethical is so vitally needed in today's world as the authors take you through a whirlwind of their experience. Understand why we must stand up for what is right while living in a

5

world filled with corrupt business and other practices that are becoming more common place every day."

- William Krol, Vice President, ABM Franchising Group, Canonsburg, Pennsylvania

"The Power of Ethics offers irrefutable and sustainable insights and principles which, when practiced, will add considerable purpose, enhanced experiences, and a framework for making difficult 'doing the right thing' decisions.

"Ethical leadership is a fascinating subject that is given life by the authors through their real-world experiences. As a result, readers will resonate with a variety of difficult situations and how they were handled, and could have been handled differently.

"In short, this book will enrich your life."

- David Summerfield, Director, Business Development, Metinvest Holding LLC, The Hague, The Netherlands, and Donetsk, Ukraine.

Acknowledgements: The two authors of this book are merely the tip of a very deep fount of knowledge about ethics, and we would be unethical if we did not acknowledge and thank at least a few of those scholars and practitioners who have come before us. We start with Plato, Aristotle, Locke, Kant, Spinoza, Mill and the many others who have grappled with the subject starting more than 2000 years ago. We continue with the many recent and contemporary philosophers in our universities who examine this fascinating, uniquely human trait that is so vital to a civil society. Many have published their insights for all to read and to develop insights of their own, and several are noted in APPENDICES G and H.

We also acknowledge and thank our contributors, all of whom broadened and deepened the perspectives of the authors and this book: Ed Collins for his profile of his lawyer that proves that 'ethical lawyer' is not an oxymoron; a top engineer who prefers to be anonymous for his anecdote concerning his dispute with his managers, demonstrating that principles are indeed important; George Dvorzak for his anecdotes concerning machine design and mine safety; Jim Browne for his comments on ethics in financial management and the Hall of Fame; Gary Forcey for his contributions to the Hall of Fame; and Don Nusser for his contributions to The Hall of Fame and the definition of ethics. We apologize to those we have inadvertently omitted.

The Authors

TABLE OF CONTENTS

INTRODUCTION:

THE PRESSING NEED TO BE MORE ETHICAL:

HAS IT ALWAYS BEEN THAT WAY?

'Ethics is nothing else than reverence for life.' Albert Schweitzer

Ethics--described briefly as the norms by which acceptable and unacceptable behaviors are measured--has been the concern, and perhaps the great dilemma, of sentient humans since Socrates subjected it to philosophical inquiry almost 2500 years ago. Socrates believed, without universal acceptance, that the most pertinent issues people must deal with are related to how we live our lives, what actions are and are not righteous, and how people should live together peacefully and harmoniously. A vast parade of philosophers, religious leaders, politicians, professors, and self-help gurus have followed Socrates' lead through the ensuing centuries; it's a popular and enduring subject, perhaps because it is so complex, intriguing, and pervasive in every facet of our lives.

Today, in 2014, ethics dominates our news in the form of anti-ethics. The headlines in newspapers and the lead stories on TV, radio, and Internet news are typically about such abhorrent behavior as lying, stealing, revenge, convictions for corruption, gratuitous murder, and misuse of public or other people's funds for personal gain. Readers, viewers, and listeners can hardly be faulted for thinking that we live in a corrupt society, exactly what Socrates and others did not want or envision. Perhaps the anti-ethical stance of the media is the most anti-ethical part of our society.

Nevertheless, the battle for a more ethical society rages unchecked and unabated; one needs only to examine the dozens of books with 'ethics' in their titles on sale at Amazon or Barnes & Noble, including this one and those that are listed in APPENDIX G. I daresay that the authors, including the two who created this book, hope that their words and thoughts will help move us toward a more civil society.

The authors are both optimistic and pessimistic: optimistic in that they see considerable interest and renewed vigor in teaching ethical behavior in our business and professional colleges; pessimistic in that they do not see our popular media either willing or able to change from reporting unethical to reporting ethical behaviors, from reporting tears and fears to reporting smiles and hopes.
Readers of this book can help. As pointed out in the prologue, all of us can be ethical ambassadors, all of us can be ethical role models: perhaps doing so is our most ethical obligation.
Regardless, it's a start.

PART I: SETTING THE STAGE

'There is no such thing as business ethics. There is only one kind ... you have to adhere to the highest standards.' Marvin Bauer, former Managing Partner, McKinsey & Company

Can business survive the scandals of the past (think ENRON, WorldCom and many others of the1990s and early 2000s and Johnson and Johnson in 2013) Can business survive the subsequent call for increased government regulation spawned by the scandals?

Of course it can--by behaving more ethically. Of course that could be a Pollyannaish hope and far too simplistic, and of course it nevertheless is possible. Is it probable? That's up to you, us, all of us in business, academe, and government. We control our own destiny.

Will we? We're optimistic that business can be conducted honestly and ethically: anecdotal and empirical evidence convinces us that an accelerating number of business and professional schools, and businesses themselves, require students and employees to complete courses in ethics and to subscribe to codes of ethics. And, beyond education, employees seem to be adopting ethical behavior at an increasing rate.

We're also pessimistic: Seventy-two of the Fortune 100 include 'integrity' or its equivalent in their statements of values; twenty-eight of them

Why?

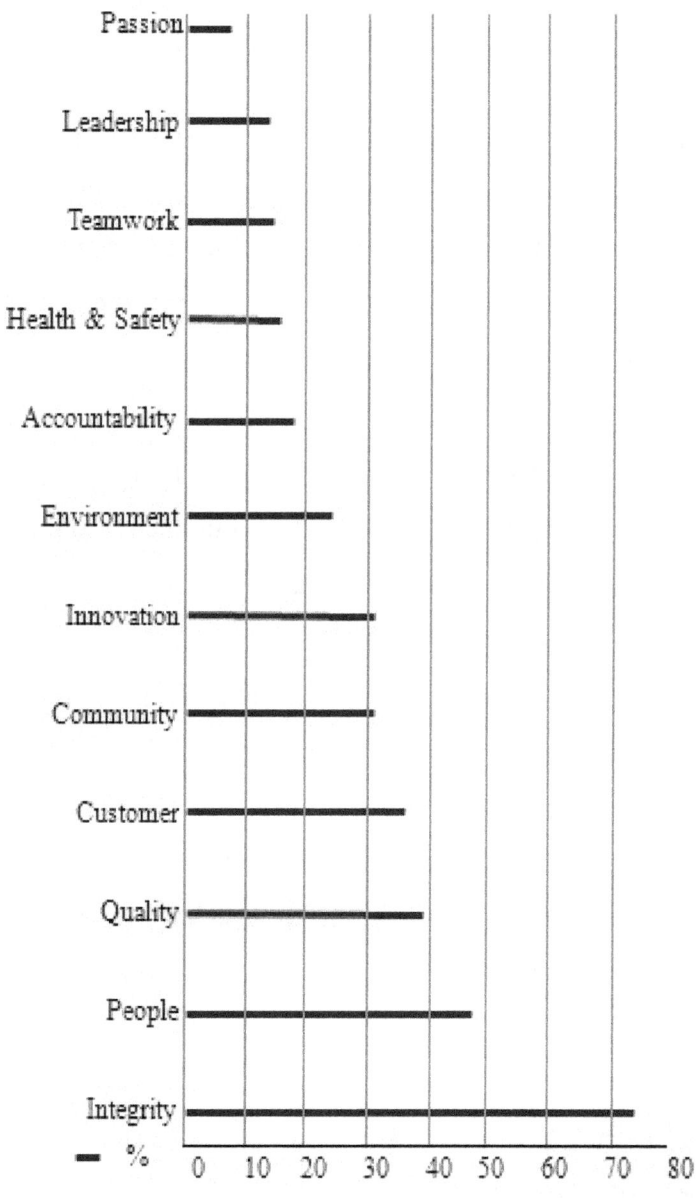

PROLOGUE: THERE'S NO PLACE TO HIDE:

AND THERE SHOULDN'T BE

'There's been a sea change in our focus on corporate ethics. We've made more progress in the last three years than in the previous thirty.' Steve Odland, former President and CEO, Office Depot, 2005--2010, and now President and CEO of The Committee for Economic Development, Washington, D.C.

Ethics--or its lack-- sticks its multi-faceted nose into just about every inter-personal activity, or it could and should. But, unfortunately, not everyone understands and practices this truism, and all too few of the folks who lead our institutions are aware of the need for ethics and have made ethical practices an integral part of their everyday activities, although we daresay that most or all say that they do, which of course is lying and, obviously, unethical. So, if ethical behavior is widely thought to be needed and is beneficial to individuals and institutions, why doesn't everyone practice it all the time?

The answer is deceptively simple: too many people, unfortunately and to their own detriment, are unaware, aka ignorant, of the need for or positive consequences of ethical behavior. On the other side of that same coin, too many people, unfortunately and to their own detriment, are blissfully unaware of the negative consequences of unethical behavior, blinded as they could be by selfishness, greed, and the need for control over others.

The operative words are unfortunately and to their own detriment. To resurrect an old catch phrase from the 1967 movie, Cool Hand Luke, "What we've got here is a failure to communicate". How can that be? Simple. We live in a clamorous world of blatant and relentless cacophony and constant time pressures that literally force us to make decisions without serious consideration of doing what is 'right'. We are bombarded with more information in one day than a person living a century ago received in a lifetime. As a result, it is all too easy to shrug off unethical behavior with those shopworn and fallacious standbys, 'everybody does it', or, 'we'll forgive it just this once'. Or we allow our busy schedules to be our excuse: it's not a good one.

All of us make choices every day, many of which have become habits – when to get up; what to have for breakfast; where to sit at the table, whether to drive to work along the same old route or take the bus – mundane stuff that provides little or no challenge in decision-making and that affect nobody but ourselves. But every now and then we make a more impactful decision – a decision that shapes our reputation and future, and those of others. For those decisions we need to be aware that ethics, consciously or unconsciously, usually –always? --plays a major part. Ethical behavior becomes habitual by routinely applying the ethical behaviors described in CHAPTER 4 and the behaviors of habitual excellence discussed in The Power of Habit by Charles Duhigg.

In addition, we need to share, with everyone who may not be as aware of the need for ethics as we supposedly are, that everyday ethics – consideration of what is the right, polite, responsible, and constructive thing to do – can have a positive or negative effect on those decisions that will remain with us for the rest of our lives. Familiar examples might be running a red light or texting while driving, endangering pedestrians and other drivers, or simply giving the finger to another driver, endangering our sense of propriety and their opinion of our manners or self control. On a positive note, simple acts such as opening the door for or volunteering to help others, and merely saying please and thank you, can enhance our image and sense of doing what's right.

Ask folks in the general public what they know about ethics and they are likely to tell you – if you get an answer at all beyond a shrug and blank stare – about a congressional committee that they've heard was censuring one of its members, or the fact that there was a recent newspaper item saying that the local hospital was forming an ethics committee (which everyone knows is a good thing), or that some executive was paid millions to sell his company or a manufacturing plant and put a bunch of workers on the street (which workers know is a bad thing but managers might know as a good thing if it was needed to save the business).

Rarely will one of them address their personal behavior except to justify it, because few of us recognize that ethics—like breathing, eating, and talking-- is something we all live with all the time. We'd all benefit if we were more keenly aware that our futures often depend on the ethics of decisions that we make as frequently as every minute.

We need to raise awareness of ethics and its antithesis, and their consequences.

We need this book: it:

… reminds us of the process of recognizing and analyzing ethical and unethical behavior, and of arriving at ethical decisions and actions that can be supported.

…illuminates our own everyday ethical decision-making via anecdotes to which readers can resonate.

...creates awareness of the human traits that encourage or discourage ethical behavior.

…demonstrates and explains the consequences of ethical and unethical behavior.

You can be an ethics ambassador; start with yourself, expand to others.

Introspection is a first step toward a more ethical society. No matter how ethical we feel that we are, we can always be more so and, by adding to our ethical maturity, we can add to our statures as role models. We suggest that at the end of each day readers asses their behavior to uncover ways they could have behaved in a more ethical manner. To continue the thought, all the anecdotes of ethical and unethical behavior could have transpired differently and, perhaps, in ways that would be considered more ethical. For example, Ford engineers, in CHAPTER 8, could have defied authority and saved lives and expensive lawsuits, and, we daresay, would have been happier with their decision.

Introspection is equally important. You encounter countless opportunities to spread the word about everyday ethics in business and elsewhere --often by your ethical behavior that supports your words. The rewards that increased awareness of ethical decision-making can bring to all of us are enormous--happiness, prosperity, sustainability, pride, peace, contentment, character and more as discussed in CHAPTER 1.

You can help spread the need for ethics: Mention ethics when you speak at employee meetings inside and outside your business ... School Board and Book Club meetings ... in letters to editors... any contacts with your elected representatives ... family gatherings ...the dinner table ... the list is endless.

Too, should the opportunity present itself, we could all be everyday ethics advocates by telling of the remarkable agreement about what constitutes ethical performance across many different world cultures. This remarkable concurrence--that honesty, respect, responsibility, fairness and compassion comprise five basic tenets of ethics--was discovered and established during research performed under Rush worth Kidder and reported in his 2005 book Moral Courage. It is a key concept, a remarkable revelation, and it deserves wide publicity.

But first, some definitions of key concepts in this book so that we understand each other as precisely as possible

Arrogance: Aggressive assertiveness, presumptuousness, aka closed-mindedness and the primary cause of unethical behavior. It often manifests itself in selfishness and self-centeredness, greed, entitlement, mendacity, and similar vile behaviors.

Ethics: The science of morals in human conduct; moral principles; rules of conduct; a set of these such as medical ethics (first do no harm) and political or societal ethics (act for the greater good). Ethics extends beyond the law and the Golden Rule, as pointed out in PART II. Please refer to APPENDIX A for additional thoughts, quotes, and quips about ethics and its intentionally broad meanings.

Ethical filter: A conscious thought process that asks if a certain situation, behavior, or response involves a conflict between good and bad, right and wrong, and our intent to address those issues.

Ethical maturity: A level of education and experience that permits ethical issues to be recognized as they arise and acknowledges that they must be addressed thoughtfully.

Humility: Humbleness, meekness, modesty, aka open-mindedness that is the antidote to arrogance and a primary cause of ethical behavior. It often manifests itself in truth, enlightenment, transparency, and similar admirable behaviors.

Integrity: Moral uprightness, honesty, truthfulness, wholeness, soundness, and the reputation for exhibiting those qualities.

Morale: the mental attitude or bearing of a person or group, especially as it pertains to confidence, discipline, or trust.

Morality: the degree of conformity of an idea, practice, etc. to moral principles.

Morals: concerned with goodness or badness of human character or behavior, or with the distinction between right and wrong; accepted rules and standards, conforming to accepted standards of general conduct. In general, ethics applies to individual behavior, while morals applies to societal/group/cultural behavior.

Value: A trait that is embraced wholeheartedly and practiced habitually because it has become part of you, like breathing, and is reflected in behavior as well as words.

Virtue: Moral excellence, goodness, uprightness.

Vice: Evil or immoral conduct, depravity, corruption on various levels of severity. E.g., a less severe vice might be smoking or overuse of alcohol or illegal drugs, all of which are unethical since they harm the user and others; more severe might be stealing from individuals or stockholders, lying about financial results, and the obvious criminal activities such as rape, murder, robbery, arson, kidnapping, and identity theft.

Ethics and ethical persons: an employee's view
What does "ethical" mean, anyway? A set of rules? Someone's

version of "doing the right thing□" Webster defines "ethical" as, in part, "following accepted rules of behavior." I have worked for a number of companies, and all have had some kind of "ethics policy" that I was (clear my throat here) "asked" to endorse with my signature. Malfeasances invariably carried the penalty of "discipline" (whips? paddles?) and of course included "up to and including termination." Parenthetically, why not just "termination"? How can you get "up to" termination and not then be terminated? Would that be like one of those faked "executions" where they hold the pistol to your head and pull the trigger ("click!") and THEN you realize the barrel was empty?

At any rate, I have signed corporate policies which usually advised me that I was going to adhere to a set of standards contained therein, which, for the most part, dealt with the obvious: no bribes, no buying jobs from clients, no buying gifts for clients, no accepting gifts from clients, no stealing company secrets, ad infinitum. They were, in fact, all things NOT to do. One exception: there was almost always a mention toward the end of the policy of one thing we SHOULD do (and is, therefore, by association, "ethical") and that is: report on any unethical behavior we observed! However, in my mind, there could (and maybe should) be a list of the hundreds of OTHER things we should do that are ethical, and would be much better proofs of our ethical nature compared to simply avoiding behavior which most of us (me,

24

anyway) would deem too risky to try – I mean, I cannot imagine myself sitting in some dark café somewhere handing over an envelope stuffed with cash under the table in order to secure my next sale.

So in addition to adhering to a set of rules you signed under implied (and possibly unethical!) coercion by your employer, what constitutes ethical behavior? Another part of Webster's definition is "…involving morally right and wrong behavior." Would it benefit us to get into a discussion over the meaning of "right" and "wrong"? Of course not, and we shouldn't, because it would be, for the most part, futile – far too many tangents and political issues. But I am sure there are many things we observe in life that a vast majority of us would agree "are the right things to do", and I can only hope that we have experienced much less behavior which we can agree "just isn't right".

So I think an "ethical" person would obviously avoid the latter, but also actively seek ways to promote and extend the former. Some do this quite well, others not. Personally, I believe that those who fail in this area of life are more observant of their own selves (How do you like this shirt I'm wearing? Did you notice my new car in the parking lot? Will this make me look good to my boss?) and less observant of the good things others do – and to take it one step further – less observant because, God forbid, they would then have to take this knowledge of good and ethical behavior and imitate it (or not).

I believe one of the keys to a happy life is to observe, and one of the things we need to observe (and remember, and imitate – I think the popular term these days is "pay forward") is the behavior of the ethical people around us. I hope your life is as filled with people doing ethical things, the right things, as mine is. You probably have hundreds of examples surrounding you: the key is to observe them and take notes. And imitate.

NOTE: The authors acknowledge the many ethical principles and theories that have been put forth by respected academicians and philosophers. We consider them too theoretical to be appropriate for a book such as this that is focused more on the practical applications of ethics and their consequences. Nevertheless, they are important to a full understanding of ethics and interested readers can dig more deeply into them via the several books on the subject that are listed in APPENDIX G. In brief, the ethical principles include:

• Beneficence guides us to do what is good;
• Least harm deals with situations in which no single choice of action is beneficial;
• Respect for autonomy allows people to control their lives and decisions; and
• Justice prescribes actions that are fair to those involved.

The ethical theories include:

- Deontology insists that people should adhere to their obligations and duties when analyzing an ethical dilemma;
- Utilitarianism is founded on the ability to predict the consequences of an action;
- Rights that are set forth by society are protected and given the highest priority;
- Casuist compares a current ethical dilemma with a previous one; *and*
- Virtue judges a person by his character rather than by an action.

CHAPTER 1: WHAT'S IN IT FOR YOU:

THE MULTIPLE AND MONUMENTAL REWARDS OF ETHICAL BEHAVIOR

'If you build that foundation, both the moral and ethical foundation, as well as the business foundation, and the experience foundation, then the building won't crumble.' Henry Kravis, co-founder of Kohlberg Kravis Roberts, a large private equity firm. The anecdotes in PART II of this book demonstrate conclusively and persuasively that ethical behavior yields three powerful and closely related benefits:

1. Happiness that is grounded in the serenity and comfort of a mind at peace with itself: We describe this desirable human condition in several ways throughout this book: Persons likely are at peace and behaving ethically if they sleep well at night, can look themselves in the mirror and be comfortable with what they see, and are as productive—able to focus on and complete the tasks at hand-- and healthy as ever. Conversely, persons are likely behaving and reacting unethically if they are confronted with a situation that keeps them awake at night, upsets their digestion, increases their consumption of drugs or alcohol, or otherwise pushes them into unusual and destructive behavior. Readers will find examples of both in this book, and, upon reflection, find examples of both in their lives.

The great thinkers agree: Aquinas, for example, points out that 'happy is he who has all he desires, provided that he desires nothing amiss.' Mill regards virtue as one of several equal parts of happiness, but Aristotle thinks that virtue is the principal means to happiness because it regulates the choices that must be rightly made; his definition of happiness is 'activity in accordance with virtue.' He also said that, 'good character is the chief determinant of happiness, itself the goal of all human doing.' Kant says that happiness should be a consequence of moral action. Freud identifies happiness with peace of mind. We could continue this chain of thought ad infinitum by citing Spinoza, Nietche, Leibnitz, and others but the point is clear: the great thinkers equate happiness with ethical behavior.

Happiness and peace of mind based on ethical behavior also result in:

2. Prosperity of individuals and businesses: To be blunt, unethical behavior is often illegal and will often lead to excessive fines or extended incarceration; witness the several accounting scandals of the late twentieth and early twenty-first centuries. Unethical behavior can also lead to loss of a job and career; witness the anecdote about the Quality Control engineer in PART II. On the other hand, ethical behavior is always within the law--it often extends beyond legal compliance-- as pointed out by Rushworth Kidder in APPENDIX B.

Corporate ethics is a primary—some would say the primary-- distinction of a business and a businessperson, a particularly important differentiation in this age when 'branding', nee 'positioning', is now considered more of a competitive advantage than ever. Ethical behavior helps assure the loyalties of employees and customers, which enhances profitability by reducing expensive turnover, litigation, business disruption, fines and the like. And, as a bonus, the public generally sees ethical behavior as positive and prefers to do business with ethical people and firms.

This trend seems to have become global: The Japan Times reported that young Japanese adults increasingly pass up promotions in the workplace. Forty percent cite the lack of ethics and the prevalence of dishonest practices as a primary reason.

A firm with a deserved reputation for treating employees fairly and generously, honoring contracts by delivering the promised quantity and quality of products and services on time, paying bills when due, donating to charities, protecting the environment, conserving energy, recycling materials-- the fundamental ingredients of behaving responsibly--is likely to be viewed more favorably. It will also be rewarded with initial and repeat business, loyal and productive employees, and positive community relationships--the essence of sustainability. On the other hand, a firm that behaves in opposite ways runs the risk of stagnation and eventual bankruptcy. In addition, ethical behavior means less government oversight, while unethical behavior guarantees more. Ergo, ethical behavior actually decreases compliance costs and increases profitability.

3. Sustainability and independence: Corporate ethics, over time, could very well be more important than profitability for businesses that want to stay in business. To see the truth behind this powerful opinion, we need to look no further than the disappearance from the corporate landscape of Adelphia, ENRON, TYCO, WorldCom, Global Crossing, Westinghouse and too many other former icons. (An interesting and provocative fact that perhaps supports the notion of sustainability: only 61 of the companies listed on the original, 1956, Fortune 500 exist today. Most were lost to mergers, but others...?).

Additional thoughts about trust, one of the several byproducts of ethical behavior: According to a 2013 Gallup poll, only 30 percent of full-time workers -- some 30 million people--are actively engaged in their work; the other 70 percent are disengaged because, they say, they do not trust their organization or boss to act in the best interests of the firm or its employees. Translated, the 70

31

percent see their managers as behaving in ways that promote their self-interest, such as juggling financial statements to increase the value of stock options or to keep their positions. The cost of this lack of trust, again according to Gallup, is $450 to $550 billion/-year, the direct result of lower productivity. On the other hand, trusting employees are willing to go the extra mile because they care.

To continue the thought: Business moves faster, i.e. more productively, when the involved parties trust each other. A simple example: I--Pete Geissler--have never had a written contract for my services simply because my clients trust me to deliver the promised product and I trust them to send me a check. Projects are started with a phone call and we bypass the several-days process of a purchase order. I have been cheated only once in 40 years. I recently purchased a new computer and the vendor wanted to create a written contract; I told him that I saw no reason to do so and we proceeded to complete the job in record time, which we could not have done if we didn't trust each other.

To further support the relationship between trust and speed: Recall the jobs you held where trust was tantamount. Chances are that there were no ulterior motives or hidden agendas, and communications were open, honest, transparent, and accessible. Time wasn't wasted explaining motives or second-guessing, and there were no meetings to discuss what the boss really meant or wanted. A possible Utopia?

Yes. It's easy to build trust and enjoy reap the benefits of greater productivity; just adopt the nine habits described in CHAPTER 4. Reverse those same behaviors and watch trust disappear and be replaced by distrust and a demoralized workforce.

CHAPTER 2: THE UNIVERSAL NEED FOR ETHICS:

BUSINESS IS THE PERFECT CATALYST

'I believe, indeed, that overemphasis on the purely intellectual attitude, often directed solely to the practical and factual, in our education, has led directly to the impairment of ethical values.'
Albert Einstein

Most--dare we say all?— professions such as engineering, law, and journalism; institutions such as government, education, and sports; and groups of people with similar interests such as Hell's Angels and companies—have adopted codes of ethics to guide, limit, restrict, and generally define expected behavior of all their members. The codes generally state that the member should 'do what's right.' The problem is that different people perceive different behavior to be 'right' at different times; more explanation is essential if the codes are to be meaningful and enforceable.

The issue of ethics is universal. All people face ethical situations in their professional and personal lives: conflicts of interest, suspicion of wrongdoing, dishonesty, theft, misrepresentation (aka lying, misspeaking, and spinning the truth), and downright chicanery and cheating, aka self-serving reasoning and the destructive actions it causes.

Business ethics refers to standards of conduct that every

stakeholder--shareholders, employees, customers, suppliers, community residents and so on--- wants and is expected to follow. It includes the notion that the person, the single entity of a business, and the far broader institution of business itself requires that members have and display a certain degree of competence before acting in a manner where others will be relying on that competence. Engineering ethics, for example, assures the public that it can rely on the technical actions or assertions of the engineer and that the result will meet the intended or represented specifications, that, for example, the bridge will not fall and the machine will operate as promised. Journalism ethics demands that the information reported be true and, in many cases, original in the sense that it is not plagiarized.

Most codes of ethics offer assurances of health, safety, reliability, environmental sustainability, quality, durability, and economy by way of fiscal responsibility--plus other desirable traits of products, services, and behaviors. Yet, many of these concepts involve

trade-offs such as planned obsolescence, cost/benefit analysis, and risk management. Nobody can guarantee 100% fitness for use forever, precise financial statements, impeccable product quality, or absolute personnel safety, for example, but everybody can adhere to generally accepted standards so that the public understands exactly what is being represented, warranted, and assured. In short, while perfection is illusive, excellence is real, possible, and the attainable goal.

Many firms, regardless of size or type, have adopted 'Values' (almost all including 'Integrity'), and their own codes of conduct.

Many have appointed Chief Compliance Officers for ethics, just as they have appointed compliance officers for law, safety, health, environmental responsibility, fiscal control, and sustainability. Some companies have created networks of Integrity Champions comprised of respected and trusted individuals who can be consulted when difficult issues arise. All employees from janitors to directors are expected to behave in accordance with those corporate values.

The core of ethical behavior is personal integrity. Individuals make choices, right or wrong, good or bad, ethical or unethical. Those choices are inevitably reflected in the organization or institution where they work.

We in business--or in any organization, for that matter-- are challenged continuously to do what is right. However, the mandate for meeting ever-rising annual and quarterly expectations for profit-ability, the stress of time and creativity in the workplace, the drive to complete every task better, faster, and cheaper, often with limited funds-- doing what is 'right' is not always the easy choice.

Still, it is always the best choice, the only choice. When Vince Lombar-di—that icon of unbending and demanding leadership in the business of sports-- famously said that 'winning is everything', he meant that winning is his and his team's only choice. We hope that he added: 'within the rules of the game'. Perhaps this admonition can invite others to entertain unethical behavior, as pointed out in CHAPTER 15, ETHICS IN SPORTS.

When persons entering the workforce ask us, the authors, to recommend and profile the best potential employer, our response is, typically, to work for a person and a company that you respect and admire for their unimpeachable ethics. We see such persons as the enlightened leaders who seek to do what's best. .. support employees to complete assigned tasks by providing them with the needed tools ... strive for the theoretical limits of what is possible...teach others how to use their imaginations...talk and act in superlatives ...never settle for 'good' or even 'better,' but always strive to
be 'best.'

In short, we believe that ethical, honest, supportive behavior is the only way to live, and we hope that readers, if they don't agree with us already, will after they read and reflect on the principles put forth in this book.

CHAPTER 3: SIX STEPS TO ETHICAL POWER:

Businesses and the jobs they create will be more sustainable and profitable if all employees—including and especially top executives -- behave ethically at all times; directors should be included, but they are typically so distant from operations that it is futile to expect them to be integral parts of the organization. The point is that ethics is a full-time job that permeates all disciplines. To that end, leaders must equip all employees with the formal process needed to clearly identify, understand, and successfully resolve ethical dilemmas.

The process will be most effective if employees:

• Empathize and resonate with relevant corporate values and anecdotes such as those in this book, all of which are derived from the real-world experiences of the authors and their associates in business; and

• Translate the theories of moral philosophy (See APPENDIX C for a brief survey of thoughts from the great philosophers) and ethical traditions into accessible and practical actions.

The infusion and habituation of ethics begins with the six R's that will become second nature after they are applied formally to two or three incidents, as we demonstrate in PART II. Some steps can be combined, some added, to fit a specific situation. Also, we suggest that readers brainstorm with a well-versed and trusted colleague or friend as they proceed through the process; it could lead to new ideas or simply reinforce your thinking and behavior.

Step 1: Recognize: If the situation makes you uneasy and queasy … if it keeps you awake at night…then you could be facing an ethical dilemma that needs to be resolved for your own happiness and peace of mind, a primary benefit of ethical behavior. Even before proceeding to the ethical reasoning strategy outlined below, please consider the insights of modern moral psychology and neuroscience; they suggest that emotional reactions are rational and relevant to moral reasoning. Unconscious perception of ethical or moral dissonance, when it bubbles up to the surface of our awareness, deserves your full attention.

Caution: While knee-jerk, gut reactions might alert you to a potential issue, acting solely on such signals may be irresponsible. In fact, research has demonstrated that blindly following one's intuition can result in less-than-optimal outcomes, and, therefore, we advise that you complement intuition with a robust, intentional, and deliberative strategy for identifying and resolving ethical dilemmas.

This first step assumes that the person taking it has the ethical maturity needed to discern ethical from unethical, right from wrong. We call on Aristotle for a description of ethical persons/-

judges, and we paraphrase and interpret:

Ethical persons, and those that judge the ethics of other persons, possess the admirable human characteristics that fit a person for life in an organized civic community, and considers how such characteristics can be fostered or created and their opposites prevented.

Consider that many people do not appreciate or recognize ethical dilemmas, and that the best teacher of recognition is experience. The authors' experiences, expressed in part by the anecdotes herein, will help.

Busy-ness is not an excuse for failing to recognize an ethics issue; it is not a reason to de-activate our ethical filters. We are all busy, some of us too busy, with long to-do lists and seemingly impossible deadlines imposed by demanding bosses and family pressures; you know them so there is no need for another list. Nevertheless, your ethical filter must over-arch all other activities. Tip: think of overwhelming busy-ness as an opportunity to pause and consult your moral compass.

Step 2: Research: Only after examining the situation--most have more than two points of view, especially when the ethical issue is unclear--and gathering the relevant facts can you begin to under-stand and articulate the precise dynamics of the issue. This step can help or hinder any resolution: It helps if the perceived ethical dilemma can be mitigated or completely resolved early and quickly, as gathering and clarifying relevant facts may reveal an inconsequential misunderstanding or missing information. It can hinder if gathering and clarifying the facts can confirm, complicate, and intensify an ethics dilemma by adding a dispute regarding the facts.

The bottom line: Commit to ascertaining as much information as possible--delegate fact-finding to a trusted associate if necessary--so that your analysis is not compromised by erroneous assumptions and blind spots and can be defended against the deepest scrutiny by third parties and the public. But move as quickly as practicable; delay can be construed as condoning the behavior in question.

Step 3: Repose: Stop, pause, and engage in circumspect and creative contemplation to discern various options for acting within a given situation and to envision the potential help and harm that are likely to result. Only then can you avoid future regrets and confrontations caused by failure to recognize and consider a full range of possible actions.

Step 4: Reconcile: Questioning the realities and consequences of your options and relating them to what's right and wrong will clarify the values and priorities implicit in your ultimate decision.

Your interrogation might be guided by examining:

IMPACTS ON OTHERS:

- Who are all the stakeholders that will be impacted by this option, and how will they be impacted? In other words, what are the foreseeable consequences of your decision on people, profits, and the planet? Does this option create shared value or will it result in a zero sum outcome?

- Does this option result in the least amount of foreseeable suffering? If harm is inevitable, does this option fairly and efficiently allocate benefits and burdens to all impacted parties?

- Are human rights, rules/regulations of your profession, corporate/organizational codes of conduct, or any U.S./international laws implicated by your decision? Is there a law, principle, or policy that simply must be followed or enforced? If so, you might be legally obligated to report the incident and its resolution.

IMPACTS ON YOURSELF:
- What duties or responsibilities do you owe to stakeholders? Do you owe a special duty to your company and/or its investors?
- Would you prefer this option if you were adversely impacted by

43

it?

- How would you feel if everyone selected this option in a similar situation? Is this option in harmony with your organization's culture and norms?

- What type of person might you become if you choose this option and ones similar to it on a continuing basis? For instance, if you want to be known as a reliable and responsible person, what would this option say about your character and integrity?

- Will you be able to look at yourself in the mirror and be comfortable with the person you see and put your head on the pillow and sleep well at night if you choose this option? What type of legacy are you creating for yourself and your organization?

- Could you defend your actions before shareholders, the Board of Directors, peers, and family?

- How would you look if this situation was completely transparent--if the facts were interpreted and reported on the front page of the New York Times, Wall Street Journal, or your local paper? Or on national or local TV news? Or on Twitter or Facebook? How would your Mother react?

Step 5. Respond: Select and implement the option that survives the rigorous investigation completed in Step 4 as the best and most rational in the sense that it minimizes impacts on others and yourself, maximizes expectations of integrity and honesty, and is consistent with your values and virtues. Be prepared to defend your choice; you may be pressed for a more rigorous explanation by others who disagree with or question your decision. If someone else is responsible for acting, recommend actions and follow up to be sure that your recommendations are considered fully and fairly. Not acting is not an option: it condones unethical behavior and sends the wrong signal to everyone in the entire organization, many of whom will be watching.

Step 6: Review. Only then can you continuously improve the process and the ethical behavior of employees and image of your organization. Ask yourself:

- Was publicity appropriate?

- Did the punishment fit the crime?

- Could the situation have been avoided with pre-emptive steps? Can you change/improve the culture/structure of your organization so that similar issues can be avoided or made less vexing in the future?

- Could you have completed the investigation more quickly, thoroughly, and fairly?

- Could you be better prepared if confronted by a similar situation in the future? Could you assure others and yourself that this situation can never be repeated?

CHAPTER 4: NINE HABITS THAT ENCOURAGE ETHICAL POWER:

INTERNALIZE THEM AND REAP THE REWARDS

'The time is always right to do what is right.' Martin Luther King

We all can benefit from greater awareness of the habits that enhance and encourage ethical behavior regardless of how ethical we perceive ourselves to be. Readers will note that each habit can be reversed to be an impediment. For example, the ethically enhancing habit #1, Practice humility, can be reversed to the ethically destructive Practice arrogance; and #4, Interpret the rules; bend them prudently but do not break them, can become the ethically destructive Break the rules when it suits your purposes.

1. Practice humility at all times; it is the source of all other habits and it prevents arrogance. Humility opens your mind to the ideas of others simply because you know that you don't have a monopoly on intelligence and insight. Paul O'Neill, former Chairman of Alcoa and the 72nd United States Treasury Secretary, in the G. W. Bush administration, is a fine example of humility: he designed Alcoa's corporate headquarters with all open offices of the same size and furnishings, including his own, to encourage openness and cross-fertilization of ideas. See APPENDIX D for more the destructive role of arrogance and the positive influence of humility, which is the essential prerequisite for habit #2…

2. Consider the consequences of your actions, which can best be demonstrated by a series of questions: Ask yourself: Would Jeffrey Skilling of the ENRON scandal—the self-appointed 'smartest man in the room'-- have cooked the books if he had known of his jail term and disgrace? Would the partners at Arthur Andersen have overlooked aggressive accounting procedures at ENRON if they had foreseen that they would destroy the company? Would a young CPA have invested and lost $250,000 to buy into a partner-ship if he had foreseen the coming scandal? Would Tiger Woods have had affairs if he had foreseen that they would cost him hundreds of millions of dollars, several years of winning on the PGA tour, and his reputation?

Not considering, or even caring about, the consequences of actions to yourself or, primarily, to others is, perhaps, the height of arrogance and it is displayed by people who are habitually self-righteous and boastful. This character flaw leads often to failure simply because it prevents objective and rational thought and debate. Nevertheless, no matter how carefully you consider the consequences of actions, you must be ready for THE LAW OF UNINTENDED CONSEQUENCES to kick in. (APPENDIX E)

Note that we are not saying 'do what's right' because otherwise you could be fined, jailed, or fired. Although they are real concerns and incentives for ethical behavior, they are not your primary incentive of creating a better world for yourself and others. Instead, consider the effects on others rather than on yourself. For example, you are more likely to kill or injure other drivers if you text while driving.

3. Challenge tradeoffs: Every ethical issue can be resolved in several ways, as is amply demonstrated by the anecdotes that follow in Part II. For example, when engineers at Alcoa and its customers determined that beryllium in an aluminum alloy added desirable properties but could deteriorate the health of workers, they cooperated with customers to evaluate and find several metallurgical alternatives that maintained the properties and eliminated the health risks-- despite the fact that the law allows a small amount of beryllium in the alloy.

4. Interpret the rules objectively; bend them prudently, but never break them. The old saying that rules are made to be broken does not apply to the rules of ethics. However, that being said, the rules are subject to interpretation, as are laws, and the interpretation must be 'fair' as judged by others inside and outside the organization.

Most businesses apparently want to comply with laws, including Sarbanes-Oxley, the Foreign Corrupt Practices Act, and others, so they publish rules and guidelines for ethics and for referring perceived ethical violations to a higher authority, usually to an ethics compliance officer or committee, the corporate lawyer or auditor, or the board of directors. The rules and guidelines should be publicized widely, as should be the results of an ethical investigation. See CHAPTER 16 for a case in point.

5. *Tell the Truth, the Whole Truth, and Nothing but the Truth: The importance of truth as part of ethical behavior can best be demonstrated by a case study:* When proposing to calculate life cycle costs, an Alcoa engineer assumed that 100 percent of the aluminum beverage containers could be recycled but only 10 percent for a competing plastic, both unrealistic assumptions that placed aluminum in a much more favorable position. The resolution required the engineer to assume current, actual recycle rates for both materials, adding integrity to the calculations and to the person and firm making them.

Skewing calculations to favor one product or situation over another is tempting, and it is endemic. For example, in preparing budgets, the preparers are often confronted with a directive from the top such as 'next year's budget must be five percent lower than last year's'. Crafty budget-makers will devote considerable time and effort to find a baseline that favors higher budgets: Examples include last year's budget or actual (or annualized) spending, or a five -year average. Regardless, it is chicanery that destroys trust, while openness and honesty build trust.

6. *Recognize and overcome implicit prejudice:* Harvard researchers analyzed data from 2.5 million tests to determine that at least 75% of test takers show a bias favoring persons who are young, rich, and white. This widespread and deep-seated form of prejudice is distinct from overt racism and conscious prejudice, of which test takers report little or none. Yet, the influence and impact of unconscious stereotyping is disturbing, for instance, on hiring and other human resource decisions, where ethical harms have been demonstrated in both research studies and courts of law. One basic rule of ethical behavior is to treat all people with dignity and respect at all times.

7. *Consider higher authorities:* Certainly authorities such as most teachers, doctors, police, and religious leaders have earned and deserve the respect needed to influence ethical behavior. However, history and studies have demonstrated that blind and steadfast obedience to authority can override ethics, sympathy, and moral conduct. The Nazis and World War II are prime examples of both individual unethical behavior (Hitler and his close advisors) and collective amoral behavior (the German Army and citizenry), too many of whom justified their cruelty as merely following orders from superiors and fear of execution. Similar but far less consequential examples abound in business: A boss at any level orders a subordinate to bribe a potential client or a government inspector with an expensive gift or lavish entertainment, or coerces an

associate to have an affair, or orders a subordinate to lower a capital authorization request to assure approval while knowing full well that the authorized amount will be exceeded. (APPENDIX F) Avoid such deceptions.

8. Consider time pressures: Business today operates at a frenetic pace, again to optimize profits; examples abound in part II. (Time is money is perhaps a more applicable and influential truth now more than ever.) Be wary of such directives, whether you are giving or receiving them, as: 'Do whatever it takes', and 'I admire risk-takers', for they can lead to hasty, short-cut decisions that could be unethical and damaging in other ways as well. Such directives infer that ethics and the law don't matter but results do, and that is dangerous in that it can lead to expedient and irresponsible behavior. The negative impacts are demonstrated in the anecdotes in PART II, and confirmed experimentally by researchers at Princeton. (APPENDIX F)

9. Avoid equating ethics with the law; they are not identical codes of behavior. Although they are overlapping codes in that we can argue that everything that is illegal is unethical, we cannot argue that everything that is legal is ethical. A quick review of The Ten Commandments reveals that only two--thou shalt not steal or kill--are illegal; the other eight strive for a higher level of behavior. Compliance with the law is the minimal standard for ethical behavior. (APPENDIX B)

PART II: BRINGING ETHICS TO THE REALWORLD:

'To see what is right and not do it is cowardice.' Confucius, Chinese philosopher, 551-479BC

We can understand ethics by examining the lives of people whose ethics are above reproach, such as the people profiled in CHAPTER 5: THE ETHICS HALL OF FAME. These are ordinary but exemplary folks living extraordinarily ethical lives.

The overwhelming majority of business people wish to and do behave ethically most of the time; nevertheless, being human, some succumb at times to a variety of pressures and behave unethically.

Top corporate officers are particularly susceptible; some bow to the wishes of stockholders and their own ambition and cook the books-- 'aggressive accounting' is today's euphemism-- as just one prominent example. Unfortunately, directors typically aren't effective monitors; they often are too far removed from routine operations where ethical breeches generally take place, too many

53

are intimidated by the authorities that appointed them, and their judgment is often clouded by friendships--which of course leads to unintentional but self-serving blindness rather than the objectivity required by their positions.

Is the perpetrator more unethical than the monitor?

The pressures, perhaps fewer and less intense, are felt at lower levels in the corporate hierarchy: the plant manager who ships inferior products in order to meet schedules and financial targets; the purchasing agent who asks for and accepts expensive gifts; the sales engineer who accepts a contract to meet sales goals knowing that the firm will lose money, and so on.

But the right decisions are possible, and truly enlightened leaders at all levels do not succumb to outside pressures; they insist on proper accounting, shipping only product that meets specifications, and so on, all to assure sustainability despite adverse ramifications.

The following anecdotes demonstrate these and other phenomena.

CHAPTER 5: THE ETHICS HALL OF FAME:

ORDINARY FOLKS, EXTRAORDINARY BEHAVIORS

"Example is not the main thing in influencing others. It is the only thing." Albert Schweitzer

It seemed so simple at the time to write this chapter: all we had to do was ask friends and associates--and ourselves--to profile the most ethical person(s) they know. Surely we all know people that we consider truly ethical.

Not so. Responses, with only a few exceptions, ranged from: "I don't know any people I consider ethical"(an engineering manager who works for the Federal Government); 'I thought I knew some people I would think of as ethical, but they proved me wrong the longer I worked for or associated with them" (an owner of a small consulting firm); "I can't think of any"(a professor and consultant to the health care industry); "I must have run into at least one during my forty years in business, but I can't think of who that might be" (a VP of a huge construction company); "It's amazing how difficult it is to identify someone truly ethical-no matter how many people you know. "(a market researcher); and "I know any number of folks who I consider to be ethical most of the time, but not all of the time." (an industrial salesperson).

Their comments and others of a similar ilk add extreme credence to CHAPTER 2, THE UNIVERSAL NEED FOR ETHICS. They also can be construed by pessimists as a sad commentary on our society, or by optimists as an opportunity for change. The authors prefer to believe that the few people who we asked to identify truly ethical folks were too demanding,--they set the bar at extraordinary heights-- and they overlooked many who should be in the Hall of Fame.

Nevertheless, several people responded quickly and positively, and their candidates for the Ethics Hall of Fame follow. Perhaps they give us all hope for a more civil society in the future.

**

TERRY FARRELL: Ethical lawyer is not an oxymoron

Integrity is a personality characteristic that is both easy to spot and equally easy to fake. A Saint and a Con Man both appear to be imbued with integrity. The proof, of course, is in the performance. For the Saint it is a natural, life-long demonstration. For the Con Man it is a costume, to be worn as needed. To discern the difference, one often needs time.

Despite the popular characterization of lawyers as an opportunistic bunch bent on bilking clients, mine was a Saint.

Terry Farrell was a country lawyer from the hard-scrabble steel town of McKeesport Pennsylvania. So was his Dad, Paul, before him. Terry's clients were middle class, mostly – steel workers early in his career, merchants, working professionals, and later blue-collar types making do with the jobs they could find as the steel mills shut down in the 1970s and 80s.

We 'inherited' Paul, and later Terry, as our attorney through my Father-in-Law, Ed, who owned a one-man real estate and insurance business in McKeesport. When he died, Paul and Terry were practicing together. Their ready help and guidance throughout the settlement of Ed's estate and the disposal of the business was so complete but seemingly so effortless that neither we nor his widow, my mother-in law, save for a few signatures, had too much to do or were left with any concerns. The business was transferred smoothly to one of Ed's friends who was in the same business. Paul and Terry took only their normal legal fees, and my mother-in-law received a very fair settlement.

After Paul died, Terry and I became friends in a business sort of way. He saw my wife and me through the passing of my moth-er-in-law and saw me through the passing of my wife. When I later married again, after 13 years my second wife passed away. Once again Terry handled the legal work. I was executor for both of their wills.

Throughout our friendship, especially during those difficult times, Terry was reassuring, positive, reliable and demonstrably confident. There was never a doubt in my mind that that he would take care of the things that needed done and give me the guidance and assurance I needed to get through.

After Terry died suddenly this past summer, at age 62, 200 folks showed up at his funeral. Another 200 or so attended a covered dish get-together along the Youghiogheny River Trail that he so loved to bike on with his little dog in his backpack. When I spoke to those who attended – and many were not just friends but also clients – to a person they expressed their love for Terry and would reinforce their admiration for his integrity. Terry was a giver. His charities were many and his ability to hear your difficulties, demonstrate his concern for them, and act to help you in your need was apparent. While it is difficult to prove integrity, with Terry, all his clients, friends, and I could see it shining out of everything he did. You know it when you experience it in someone, and you believe it when it is unwavering.

- Ed Collins, Former Marketing Communications Manager,

**

ED LORE/LANERE COFFEE: Honesty to the max

Sometimes when digesting the news of the latest corporate skull-duggery, I force myself to remember that the vast majority of businesspersons--I've heard estimates as high as 98 percent-- do 'the right thing' as they and society see it. I also force myself to think of the hundreds of businesspersons who crossed my active and winding path during more than forty years as a consultant; they confirm 'vast majority'; almost all are ethics devotees, a few aren't and I fear won't ever be, and I've drummed them out of my life; and a handful are hybrids in the sense that they strayed temporarily and then found their way back into the fold.

Therefore, I find it unfair to crown one person out of hundreds in my life as 'most ethical ', and must wimp out and name several contenders. I've never forgotten Ed Lore, a VP at Dravo Corporation where I worked as a fledgling sales engineer in the 1960s, almost fifty years ago as I write this. I was only a few weeks into my tenure there when I was sent to a conference in New York City and told to mingle and learn. I did, and was later appalled at my generosity with Dravo's money when, a week later,

I filled out my expense account, so I decided to eat some of the cost. I still do not know how, but Ed saw what I did, called me into his office, and told me in no uncertain terms that I was to be honest with my expenses, I was not to cheat the company or myself, and to submit another report. I was stunned by his candor, but not for the first time.

A year or so later, I was negotiating a large contract and was told by my client that the job was mine if I purchased a large piece of equipment from his favorite supplier; I suspected nepotism or cronyism at work. Although the equipment was acceptable but not the first choice of our design engineers, Ed immediately refused the offer, saying that Dravo could not be coerced. We won the contract anyway.

Then, a few years later, when I decided to leave the company, Ed took me to lunch at his favorite club and told me how disappointed he was and asked if he could do anything to change my mind. When I told him that I was committed and would feel very guilty if I reversed course at this late date, he told me that he respected my stance and wished me well.

If trust is the basis for ethics, then I must nominate my long-time maid for the Hall of Fame, Lanere Coffee. When she first started to work for me, I noticed that the day after she did her thing that I would find a quarter near the phone and asked her where it came from. Seems that if she made a call she'd insist on paying for it. When I told her it wasn't necessary, she nodded in agreement and went on leaving the quarter anyway. And, BTW, she had a key to my home and could enter anytime but rarely did unless I was here.

- Pete Geissler

**

BILL O'ROURKE, SR.: If I didn't pay for it, I don't want it

My Father, Bill O'Rourke, Sr., and my mother raised a family of six children. My father was a high school teacher and coach who, during the Summer, was the Recreation Director of my small hometown. As part of his job, he would purchase a significant amount of recreation equipment from the local sporting goods store. One Saturday morning the owner of the store pulled into our home driveway where I was washing the family car and placed a new set of golf clubs in the garage, saying, 'Tell your Dad that's for him'.

My Dad was a casual golfer who played with outdated clubs; he could surely use the new set.

Later, I showed Dad the new clubs. He quickly put them in the trunk of our car and said: 'Come with me.' We drove to the store and Dad walked in with the clubs, set them at the cash register, and told the owner: 'I didn't pay for these.' Dad never talked about the incident during the drive to or from the store; he didn't need to: his actions spoke volumes about the man he was.

He was my excellent role model throughout his life. I asked him once why he never used profanity, and he replied that people who do so degrade themselves and display their limited vocabulary. He volunteered in our community, in the church, and in the neighborhood. He was respected by the many students he taught and coached and by the community, friends, relatives, and neighbors. He cared for my Mother throughout her last illness better than any nurse could. Perhaps most importantly, he was extremely content and happy, surely one of the many benefits of an ethical life.

When in high school my Dad gave me a small, handmade plaque. On it he had written: 'I don't have much to give you, but I give you my good name. I give it to you untarnished and I ask to keep it that way.'

Nobody could ask for a greater gift. I only hope that I have lived up to his high expectations.

- Bill O'Rourke, Jr.

**

JOE RESEARCH: Take this job and shove it

I resigned from my job as Research Technical Advisor for a large manufacturer of electrical equipment over an ethical dispute that I felt—and still feel—has cost homeowners millions of dollars and has lulled them into a false sense of safety as well.

The dispute centers on circuit breakers, those small devices that are installed in a steel box—once called the fuse box-- that is typically in a home's, apartment's, or a commercial building's basement or mounted in an unobtrusive wall, such as in a closet or behind a kitchen cabinet. Tens of millions of breakers are sold and installed every year. Their function is to prevent fires, deaths, and electrical shocks by tripping, i.e. turning off the electricity to an appliance such as a refrigerator or computer should there be a malfunction in the wiring to or in the appliance itself.

Annual sales of breakers amount to hundreds of millions of dollars that are divided among four manufacturers. I worked for one. .

A bit of history: The first generation breakers were designed to trip in response to overloads (too many toasters e.g.) or over-currents (short circuits, lightning strikes, e.g.). The second generation added electronic personal ground fault circuit interruption GFCI (protection against shock and electrocution).

Today there is a third generation that provides protection against the so called 'arcing fault'. These faults are the result of insulation failures caused by a very high current that is sporadic, called parallel arcing faults. A normal breaker will not respond to such faults; a new electronic breaker design is required. Such a breaker was available-- they were called Arc Fault Circuit Interrupters (AFCIs)—but aren't now. Today a newer type of device called a Combination AFCI is avail-able and is legally required in new homes. Manufacturers claim they provide both parallel and series arc fault protection; they are more expensive than the earlier and now disallowed devices. The industry claims that series arcing faults are a common home fire hazard and a Combination AFCI will respond and trip in response to them.

Both claims are false, perhaps even fraudulent. If a home owner asked the manufacturer to demonstrate its claims, it couldn't.

The ethical problem is that it doesn't protect as claimed by the manufacturers and by the very organizations—the dictatorial industry committees that are tasked with verifying such claims and specifying the type of breaker that must be installed in various circuits.

A bit more history: One of the four manufacturers—perhaps the most active and influential member of the industry commit-tees—contrived a laboratory demonstration to simulate an arc that may cause a fire. However, the simulation used conductors made of carbon that are never installed in homes or other buildings, rendering the simulation misleading and irrelevant. That surely is unethical.

When I pointed this out to the committee, I was told that I was picking nits and the simulation was close enough to real conditions to be valid. So I created my own simulation in the basement of my home using the identical copper conductors that are installed in just about every home and building in America.

I could not create a series arc, even under extreme conditions. Therefore, we, the manufacturers and committees, had created a non-existent problem for which we devised an expensive solution: The combination breaker. It protects against high voltages, as did fuses and the original breakers, but not against series arcs, as claimed in the literature published by each of the manufacturers.

Nevertheless, the industry committees endorsed the earlier demonstration and rejected mine, then revised its codes to require combination breakers in specified circuits in all new construction and in all renovations. That single action literally doubled each manufacturer's revenue derived from circuit breakers at the very consider-able risk of facing legal charges of fraud, which, if ever filed by homeowners, could cost each manufacturer billions of dollars.

When I pointed this out to my executive board—the marketing, legal, and top management of my employer--its members voted to 'not rock the boat.' I was so disillusioned with their blind and self-serving lapse of ethics that I packed my evidence in my brief-case and resigned on the spot, then left the building without so much as cleaning out my desk. I haven't returned, and lost several years of employment at a job I loved. But I sleep better.

I continue the battle because I know it's the right thing to do. I've recommended to industry committees one change to the codes that reflect the true conditions in buildings: delete 'combination' in the requirement for circuit breakers. That one change would save homeowners billions of dollars per year. I also present my case at industry conferences, and I maintain a website that addresses the issue.

Joe R is a former research engineer and is now a crusader for truth in technical communications concerning safety and economy in circuit breakers.

Note from the authors: Most employees will be confronted with two decisions to leave a job for ethical reasons during their careers. How they handle those decisions is a clear reflection of their true character. For example, I was asked by the Director of Communications at Westinghouse to write a series of essays on various business issues, one of which I still consider unethical: managing for stockholder value. I refused to write it and lost the entire contract and many thousands in fees. I still do not regret my decision.

**

A POTPOURRI: Identifying ethical behavior isn't easy

How little we really know of each other. This is where my mind takes me each time I begin thinking on the question of naming ethical persons. We know business associates in particular in only one facet of their lives. Unless the business relationship has blossomed into a full friendship we know so little. Sometimes friends can surprise you when you enter a financial relationship: you feel you see a side you had never seen before, and they see a side of me that they had never seen before.

Mike is an attorney that I have worked with for many years. His billing, his objectivity, his counsel, I truly respect. I know whatever the amount of work I send his way will be done quite well and at a cost that clearly has 'no hours padded.' I have been extremely comfortable with that for many years. This is a very valuable relationship professionally, and yet I know him in no other context. Sad.

Chuck was a friend and a client for many, many years. I trusted him implicitly. He was a very successful business man with many ventures. He was in fact trusted and respected among many groups and in many different contexts. He was just one of those exceptional people. Yet I knew of one transaction in one business that was absolutely legal and ethical but not quite the way I would have wanted someone to deal. Does that disqualify him in my mind? Maybe it was his partners that forced that one issue. I will never know. Bob is a college professor. Tenured and comfortable, he still works very hard over long hours; I cannot imagine anyone who works harder in such a secure position. His theme is clearly quality and delivery of a superior level of education. Difficult to imagine anyone or any purpose as more ethical.

Choosing the most ethical person is a most difficult task. Many qualify, and choosing one would be to deny the reality of the limitations of our knowledge. I could go on and on and even add a writer I know who would certainly fit into these categories. The human species has an abundance of good and bad.

- Jim Browne, Founding Partner, Allegheny Financial Group

**

MARK SCHMIDT: If the document isn't for me, destroy it

I met Mark Schmitt almost twenty years ago and I am still amazed at his honesty and integrity. I recall when he received an electronic copy from an industry trade association that was meant for a competitor and contained sensitive information that could have given Mark a competitive advantage. After reading one or two lines he realized the error, shredded the document, and notified the trade association of the error.

Mark works as a Product Manager at a large manufacturer of electrical equipment, where I worked as a Marketing Communications manager. Unlike other product managers, he responded quickly and politely to my requests for information to support marketing claims in ads, brochures, and other sales documents. He volunteered to proof catalogs and instruction manuals for their technical accuracy.

If being polite, civil, and responsible are signs of ethical behavior, as is pointed out elsewhere in this book, then Mark deserves the title of most ethical person. I have never heard him raise his voice or talk down, belittle, or berate others, and I have never seen him be impatient. And--to move from business to personal--I have never seen him play outside the rules on the golf course during the dozens of rounds we have played together, and I have never heard him cuss, reminding me of Bill O'Rourke's Father.

Politeness, fairness, integrity, honesty--that's Mark in the office, on the greens, and ,I'm sure, in every part of his life.

- Gary Forcey, former Marketing Communications Manager, Eaton Corporation.

**

KAREN WIFE/ AMANDA SMITH: Ethics in the home and office

Here's an example of how I think ethics in other than the business setting was recently demonstrated by my wife Karen. The vast majority of us can agree that it is 'wrong' and 'unethical' to abuse our domestic animals and pets. So as long as we don't go around abusing animals, we're ethical, right? Let's take it a step further.

Our 93-year-old friend and neighbor, Frank, who lived in the farmhouse ½ mile down our road, passed away last September. He left behind three outside cats who were left to fend for themselves except for the compassion of a couple of neighbors (Frank's family is in the process of trying to sell the house – cats included – but they live 500 miles away). Karen is one of those with compassion for the cats (and, by the way, we are tried and true dog people, although we own three cats ourselves, a contradiction which bears explaining, but not here).

Frank's felines were especially appreciative of Karen's attention during what turned out to be the worst winter in Pittsburgh in the past 25 years. You see, during those sub-zero nights and single-digit days, Karen would heat bricks in the oven, wrap them in a blanket, and put them under the back steps where the cats slept, giving them the life-saving warmth they needed. This gesture was not easy for her, given her responsibilities at home and the cumbersome arthritis in her hands that was exacerbated by the sub-zero temperatures.

So was that the moral and right thing to do? Yes! Ethical? Yes! And that is one of thousands of things I've observed Karen do for over these past four decades because they were 'the right thing to do.' They were the moral and ethical thing to do – all in the absence of personal gain. The things she did, and continues to do daily, show that she cares. She is truly worthy of the ethical hall of fame.

What if we consistently applied that level of doing the right thing into our everyday business? I have a friend (let's call her Amanda) who worked for a company which 'paid out' any vacation time leftover at the end of the year. A few weeks into the new year, Amanda noticed from her automatic deposit statements that she received her amount due. The following month, while reconciling her bank statements, she noticed another payout equal to the first. Amanda thought that the leftover vacation time may have been paid out over two payments, but after further evaluation, she found that was not the case. She emailed her friend Laura in the accounting department, and asked that she check the payout. She received a semi-terse email in response (which she attributed to Laura's overwhelming workload) which merely stated that the payout is correct.

Amanda could have left the matter alone, and taken the windfall with the assurance from Laura that the payout was correct However, when Amanda visited the headquarters office a few days later, she went to the accounting department and stood in Laura's door-way and said, 'I don't want to be a pain, but...'

Laura accommodated Amanda's obsession with her vacation

payout and went into the program again. Numbers scrolled across the screen as she examined the database, and she suddenly exclaimed "Oh [expletive]!!". Laura discovered that Amanda had indeed been paid twice, and her split second moment of horror resulted from her wondering just how many employees had been overpaid. Laura's next statement was shocking to both Amanda and me. Laura said, 'you know, I really appreciate you telling me about this and making me look twice, because I am sure if it was someone else, they would have kept quiet and kept the money.'

Those words resounded within me. I realized then that ethics was at work, the soft side of ethics, the 'do the right thing' ethics. The actual dollar amount was not huge, by any means, but Amanda did the right thing, the honest thing.

What if everyone practiced the soft side of ethics, as I like to call it, in the workplace on a daily basis. By that I mean being honest (as Amanda demonstrated); showing respect and extending business courtesy toward one another; telling the truth; being discrete. Let me repeat myself: we need to consider 'ethical behavior' as including a healthy dose of honesty and respect and courtesy and discretion!

I suggest that all of us inform someone about events which will impact them. Answer that email, even if it is distasteful. Keep that

73

confidential information to yourself. Give others credit when and where it is due. Lend a hand. Refrain from pulling rank. Don't throw others under the proverbial bus for your own personal gain. Do these because they are the right things to do, regardless of personal gain. I would encourage you, dear reader, to bring real ethics, not just paper policies, to the workplace. Be an example of what it takes to get nominated to the Ethics Hall of Fame!

- A Vice President of a global engineering firm who prefers to remain anonymous.**

ABBY ANONYMOUS: Going the extra mile

Abby managed the payments department for a large utility and did it very well. Each business day, she and her 10 direct reports processed thousands of check payments and deposited hundreds of thousands of dollars in the company's bank accounts with an error rate that approached zero, accelerating cash flow and lowering costs. She was publically recognized often by top managers and trade associations for her department's efficiency and employee loyalty.

She was nonplussed one day by a payment made with a deposit slip instead of a check that was obviously written by a shaky hand. So, instead of merely mailing the slip back to the sender--the first and easiest step set forth by company policy--she decided to take the next step. It was also sanctioned by company policy when she sensed unusual conditions, in this case a customer in distress.

She first called the customer, who informed her that she had run out of checks and decided to send a deposit ticket. Knowing this was unusual behavior, Abby then contacted the company's local representative and asked that she examine the customer's records for an authorized third party contact. The representative did and contacted the third party, her son, who lived 500 miles away. She learned that the son had called his Mother only a few days before and she, the Mother, said that she was in fine health and functioning well. However, upon further investigation, the son discovered that his mother had suffered a slight stroke and she had neglected paying other bills and other important matters. He immediately arranged for visits by a doctor and other caregivers and flew home to care for his Mother.

Abby's actions very likely helped the Mother and her son avoid considerable inconveniences by sensing an abnormal situation and acting quickly to resolve it. She went the extra mile, all within company guidelines, and, as she told the story to others, she focused on the prudence of having an authorized third party contact. The son sent Abby a letter thanking her and the company for doing the right thing.

**

BILL X: ETHICS ISN'T NEGOTIABLE

Bill X was the general manager of a division of a large conglomerate that manufactured electrical equipment. Bill's Marketing Man-ager, let's call him Joe, was revered for his business savvy and was relied on by many in the division to resolve all sorts of knotty problems. He and Bill became close personal friends as well as business associates.

The business was operating smoothly until Bill received an anonymous tip that Joe was taking kickbacks from a supplier ; he then investigated the tip thoroughly and verified its truth. Bill confronted Joe, who was smart enough to know that what he was doing violated the company's code of ethics and not dispute the charge. Perhaps he thought that his candid reaction and relationship with Bill would save his job.

It didn't. Bill fired Joe on the spot, Joe cleaned out his desk and was out the front door, and Bill appointed a new marketing manager--all within an hour.

Bill demonstrated to all his thousands of employees that he

expected ethical behavior at all times. As a result, Bill was respected by all who knew and worked with him, including his superiors who promoted him to positions of increasing responsibility.

- Jim G, an observer, employee, and friend.

CHAPTER 6: CREATING AN ETHICAL ORGANIZATION:

PRINCIPLES AND GUIDELINES FOR EVERYMAN

'If ethics are poor at the top, that behavior is copied down through the organization.' Robert Noyce, inventor

An important factor--perhaps the most important factor-- in creating and maintaining an ethical culture in individuals, professions, or organizations is the tone that is set by leaders at all levels--not a simple task. Executives tend to be driven and charismatic persons who push for better and better results, as they should. But in their leadership roles they must also set the tone and standard for integrity. That 'tone at the top' must be audible and visible: leaders must articulate their clear expectations, set the example by being the example, walk the talk, and train the next generation of leaders to assure that the culture continues long into the future. That is the rationale for the subtitle of this book: The Thinking Leader's Model for Sustainable Competitive Advantage.

A good example is Paul O'Neill, CEO at Alcoa for 13 years (1987-2000). He personally championed workplace safety, and it worked: The lost workday incident rate (incidents per 200,000
work hours) fell from 1.86 to 0.20 during his tenure, and it continued to fall long after he retired to 0.082 in 2013. His legacy

endures as a visionary and compassionate leader who had strong values and got results.

Honest, open communications are imperative for the subtitle to fulfill its promise. Author and Lecturer Mary Gentile, from Babson College, stresses the importance of a corporate culture that allows and even encourages employees to speak up on ethical issues, assuring that employees are heard and respected. We recommend her book: Giving Voice to Values: How to Speak Your Mind When You Know What's Right (2010).

The authors find it self-evident that building an ethical organization starts with leaders who set a high ethical bar and expect all employees to meet or exceed it, starting with themselves. Toward the end, forward-thinking leaders:

• Write a code that clearly and explicitly defines expectations for behavior while representing the firm;
• Communicate the code explicitly in writing and speaking, and implicitly by behaviors at all times that can be emulated by all employees; it bears repeating that the tone of ethics is set at the top and filters down to all employees.
• Reinforce the message with seminars and the like that are part of the policy for continuous learning, and by rewarding ethical

behavior with public pronouncements and promotions.

• Discourage unethical behavior with firings, deferred promotions, poor performance reviews, and, in extreme cases, legal action. A typical corporate ethics code covers the following topics:

1. Policy
2. Health and safety
3. Employment practice
4. Foreign Corrupt Practices Act
5. Financial reporting
6. Illegal payments
7. Conflicts of interests
8. Supplier and customer relationships
9. Political activities
10. Trading in securities with insider information
11. Protection of corporate property, including intellectual property
12. Reporting ethical violations/compliance officer

Perhaps the Code of Ethics adopted by the American Society of Civil Engineers is a good model for all or many individuals and businesses. The code stipulates that engineers must:

Hold paramount the safety, health and welfare of the public and strive to comply with the principles of sustainable development in the performance of their professional duties.

Perform services only in areas of their competence. Issue public statements only in an objective and truthful manner.

Act in professional matters for each employer or client as faithful agents or trustees, and shall avoid conflicts of interest.

Build their professional reputation on the merit of their services and not compete unfairly with others. Act in such a manner as to uphold and enhance the honor, integrity and dignity of the engineering profession and act with zero-tolerance for bribery, fraud, and corruption.

Continue their professional development throughout their careers, and shall provide opportunities for the professional development of those engineers under their supervision.

Most sizable companies have written codes of ethics; however, in the authors' experiences, many of those same companies fail to communicate or enforce its expectations adequately and the codes do not meet their purpose, perhaps because at times the codes are vague, misguided, unenforceable, or ignored by the very executives who should set the standards.

For example, The Code of Business Ethics and Conduct published by a huge manufacturer is misguided: It mixes and confuses ethics, morality, and law starting with its first sentence: '...our policy is to comply with all laws...and to conduct our affairs with the highest moral, legal, and ethical standards.' What does that mean to the average employee?

The Code continues: 'Even where the law does not apply, applicable standards of ethics and morality relate to our activities and require the same diligence and attention to good conduct and citizenship.' Would that statement mean the same to some employees in Australia as it does to those in the Middle East? More explanation is needed.

If surveys can be believed, a whopping 77 percent of American adults don't trust lawyers to tell the truth, a simple act when compared to the broader concept of ethics. Therefore, it's easy to say that mixing law, ethics, and morality is a major contradiction. And 'Even where the law does not apply...' places the law above ethics and morality, exactly where it shouldn't be. So the managers who say, 'I don't care if it's ethical. Is it legal?' are merely following the directive from above. At the same time, they are violating at least two of the nine habits for ethical power listed in CHAPTER 4, Consider Higher Authorities and Avoid Equating Ethics and the Law.

The contradictions in The Code between words and actions continue. A few examples: 'Employees shall not request or accept monetary loans or personal services from suppliers...'Employees may not accept gifts or gratuities...with the exception of advertising novelties of a nominal value marked with the donor's company name.' Pete Geissler knows better: 'I lost count years ago of the many golf games, fancy dinners, tickets to shows and so on that I gave my clients and their spouses, and that they accepted without a second thought. My competitors did the same. Is this wrong? For them? For me?'

Bill O'Rourke answers with 'yes, it was wrong': 'I managed the procurement organization for Alcoa, and was responsible for purchasing some $18 billion worth of goods and services per year. During my tenure, I was offered ski trips to Colorado, golf trips to Hawaii, and tickets to sporting events such as boxing matches, the Super Bowl, and the Olympics. I rejected all: Alcoa does not do business that way and requires that every gift, regardless of value, must be disclosed; that I must buy the supplier a meal for every meal paid for by the supplier; and there must always be a clear business purpose for every event. I asked buyers to disclose every gift, regardless of value; (Alcoa permitted gifts of 'nominal value') and expect scrutiny.

'I also was on the sales side of the business for another company. In trying to increase revenue and profitability I structured contracts that offered significant discounts for volume, a win-win. My first offer was to a mine operator who said that he would increase his purchases if I would buy his wife a Cadillac. She's still waiting.' In truth, we as a society have made ethical and legal synonyms, just as we have made unethical and illegal synonyms, and the reason is clear in my mind: it's simpler. Our laws are spelled out in huge volumes found in countless public and private libraries, and they— the laws-- are interpreted every day by judges who are almost always lawyers themselves, and are supposedly fair and unbiased.

The laws and interpretations are written to avoid ambiguities, so they are, in theory, clear. They aren't totally, of course; if they were, we wouldn't need so many lawyers and judges to continuously interpret them. As further proof that we have meshed ethical and legal, many firms have appointed a Compliance Officer to whom employees can ask questions about ethical behavior and report ethical misconduct; the officers are predominantly in the corporate legal department.

On the other hand, ethics is spelled out by the Bible, the Koran, and similar books published by countless religions. The books are written in extremely vague and abstract terms that are often contradictory, and therefore have been interpreted continuously by theologians based on their personal biases and beliefs. In addition, their interpretations are typically not written; they're spoken in sermons and homilies, so they are not usually accessible to the public.

The confusion between legal and ethical, and the emphasis on legal, is demonstrated further in The Code mentioned above: The words ethics and morality appear exactly six times (and not once after page two) in its 27 pages; the word legal and its variations appear 34 times. In addition, one chapter is entitled Illegal Payments; no chapter title mentions ethics. It's so easy to transfer our responsibilities for ethics to the lawyers, who gladly accept the extra work. Personal responsibility, especially when it comes to ethical behavior, cannot be outsourced; we own it.

CHAPTER 7: CREATING AN ETHICAL ORGANIZATION IN A HOSTILE ENVIRONMENT:

BILL O'ROURKE'S EXPERIENCE IN RUSSIA

"A leader leads by example, whether he intends to or not." Anonymous

I arrived at the Sheremetevo Airport in Moscow early in February, 2005, my first time in Russia. It was cold; both the weather and my welcome. After clearing customs, a very time-consuming process, I gathered my one, large checked bag. An airport clerk approached me and told me that my luggage was overweight. He led me to a nearby scale and asked me to put my luggage on it. I was allowed to carry 50 pounds (22.5 kilograms). I knew my luggage was under the limit. The clerk advised me that I owed fifty U.S. dollars, cash, they didn't accept credit cards. He instructed me to put fifty dollars inside my passport and hand it to him.

Sometimes our personal radar tells us that something is amiss. My radar was ringing. I had traveled extensively and knew that it was appropriate to weigh luggage when departing, not when arriving. Also, why would I put money in my passport? (I later learned that airport extortionists were sometimes watched by surveillance cameras and would often try to keep improper payments hidden from the cameras, fearing, I presume, that they'd be coerced to share the take.)

Beside me, an American woman was putting her money inside her passport. She handed it to her clerk. I said that I knew my luggage was not overweight. I asked why it was being checked on arrival. The clerk claimed not to understand my English. I asked to see someone in authority. He raised the volume of his voice, and demanded that I pay him, now. I continued to resist. He eventually walked away, never to be seen again. I grabbed my luggage and proceeded into the airport.

Welcome to Russia.

Alcoa had just acquired a downstream aluminum manufacturing business in Russia. The acquisition included two extremely large manufacturing plants; one in Samara and one in Belaya Kalitva. The acquired organization had a large Administrative and Sales office in Moscow. The CEO of Alcoa called and advised me that the negotiations had been concluded and he would like me to go to Russia as the first President of Alcoa-Russia. He added 'but I know you won't go.' I asked for 24 hours to consider it and came back the next day and accepted the position. The CEO's response was interesting: 'That's great, now I think you have no judgment; nobody in their right mind would take this job.'

Why would Alcoa even go to Russia? The per capita consumption of aluminum in Russia in 2005 was about 5 kilograms per person. Consumption in the Western world was closer to 30 kilograms per person. Alcoa saw considerable upside potential primarily in the areas of aluminum sheet for making beverage containers and for making parts for the aerospace industry.

Alcoa paid $257.5 million for this acquisition and knew that almost $1 billion would have to be invested to upgrade the facilities. The facilities had been neglected since perestroika – about 13 years. There had been no capital investment and little maintenance. The facilities were a mess (over 40,000 tons of steel scrap were removed in the first six months), and safety was a disaster (incident rates were ten times higher than the Alcoa average; fatalities were common and accepted). Just think of the issues that needed to be addressed: Language, Culture, Politics, Customer Relations, Product Quality, Government Relations, Economics (currency, duties, tax, markets, & pricing), Bureaucracy, Corruption and Security. I knew this was going to be an adventure.

I decided to live in the city of Samara, where Alcoa's largest plant in the world was located. This plant sat on 388 acres, it had 129 buildings, it had over 8,000 employees, it had the largest forging press in the world, the largest extrusion press in the world, a five-stand rolling mill and many other manufacturing facilities. I was assigned a driver. On my first trip to the Plant the local police (militia) stood on the side of the road and waved a wand at our car. I asked my driver what's happening. I learned that there is a practice of pulling over drivers and detaining them until they pay the police a few hundred rubles (at that time 1 dollar was about 30 rubles).

The police asked for papers: driver's license, insurance certifications, ownership documents, inspection documents, etc. The police looked for something out of order. If they found something wrong they demanded higher payments. If they don't find anything out of order they keep reviewing until the driver offers some money. I instructed my driver to have all his papers in order because we're not paying, regardless of how long we get detained. I'm proud to say that for the three years I lived in Russia we never paid these police. We were stopped regularly, yes, but we wouldn't pay. I was trying to set the example.

The culture in Russia is that if you have power of any kind you use it to your pecuniary advantage. I saw this often. I would travel around Russia. I was recognized as a foreigner. It was common for me to be singled-out at the airport and be detained. I refused to pay. My detainers would suggest that I could go to the banking machine, withdraw a few thousand rubles, give it to the guard and go on my way. I refused. My longest detention was nine hours in the Rostov Airport.

I heard about extortion in other areas: emergency room doctors trying to make ends meet extort their patients, even university administrators extorting the parents of college applicants and rewarding them with acceptance in return for a few thousand rubles.

I understand that the Russian government has recently increased the compensation for the militia and have asked them to refrain from their petty extortion and it has been reduced somewhat. I would like to interject that we can't be too hypocritical. In the US it was common a century ago to extort. It is still a practice in certain sections of certain cities. The Russians have only been 'free' for a couple decades. Let's give them a little more time to right their ship.

The first year that I was in Russia I had a capital budget of $100 million. I spent only $20 million. Why? Because I wouldn't pay all the people across the supply chain and all the bureaucrats in positions of authority who demanded something extra for themselves. If you don't pay, the supply chain slows down, dramatically. Much of what we bought had to move through local Import-Export Offices. Goods don't get released unless those in authority get paid. We wouldn't pay.

We brought substantial capital equipment into Russia on multiple trucks. One time the mayor and militia stopped the trucks and said 'I see so much investment coming through my city, and I'm not getting anything.' The mayor said the trucks don't move until he gets $25,000 US dollars. We didn't pay. Luckily, he let the trucks go about 72 hours later. We had this type of interference every-where. As another example, the Tax Collector showed-up at the plant. He said that he must audit the tax records; 'or you can pay me $5,000 US dollars and I'll go away.' He was told to audit the books.

I wouldn't condone or participate in the corruption. I would periodically complain to the Federal Russian Government about the behavior we were seeing in the Regions. The government wanted foreign investors, especially Alcoa, to be successful. They saw our direct foreign investment in Russia as an opportunity to attract additional investment, and it did: Alcoa's can sheet manufacturing investment in Samara (where the 'best' can sheet coating line in the world is now located) attracted other can-making companies such as Rexam, CanPack, and Ball to consider Russia for their can-making plants. By sticking to our values, by resisting the illegal demands we sent the message that we will not participate in unethical behavior. That message eventually got communicated and understood. Alcoa's investment was over $100 million in the second year and even higher in the third year.

Let me note that about half of my personal bonus was based on making the capital investments happen in Russia. When they didn't happen, I was not rewarded at year end. Selfishly, it would have been easy to make the payments to the authorities. My personal compensation would have been higher. Did my boss reward me for sticking to the values, having the personal conviction to bring Alcoa's integrity to the operation in Russia and did he choose not to penalize me because I stuck to my beliefs and values? He didn't. The Russian Plants were very inefficient. We knew that many employees would be laid-off. In fact, the number of total employees was reduced from over 15,000 on my arrival to under 8,000 when I left three years later.

In preparing for lay-offs we reviewed the company's severance policy – there was none. Under Russian law the employees were entitled to about 3 week's pay if they lost their job. Under Alcoa's compensation policy we decided that three month's pay was more fair to these employees. The HR Manager said she would handle layoffs. The way she handled it: she would call employees to her office and advise them that their job was being eliminated. She said they would get either 3 week's pay or 3 month's pay and it was up to her. She told them that if she gave them 3 month's pay she expected a kick-back. Incredible! We were extorting our own employees!

I investigated, learned it was happening and the HR Manager was released. (She didn't get 3 week's or 3 month's pay!) I asked our General Council if we should bring an action against her as we would do in the U.S. He said no, that no judge or jury would find much wrong with what she did. That's an indication of how Deep-rooted the corruption culture is in Russia. Should we make the extorted employees 'whole'? Sure, so we asked who was extort-ed. Not all were extorted, but all of them said they were. Again, that's the culture.

In the sales area, as in most areas, there was a lot of room for improvement. Pricing of our products didn't seem to follow a rational cost-plus approach. The entire price list required review and revision. I visited a number of customers. On an early visit a customer wanted to know if I wanted the same 'arrangement'. I inquired further. Evidently, it was common practice for our company to sell the product at a significant discount. The customer would be rewarded by his employer for negotiating such a great discount. Then, the customer would send a portion of that discount to the salesperson as a personal reward. Incredible.

I was an intended victim of a rather elaborate scheme in Moscow.

I was taking a walk one evening and wandered off the main streets. A man walked past me and dropped a transparent bag, in which I could see a roll of U.S bills. Within seconds of the drop I had picked up the bag, ran and caught the man who dropped it and gave it back. Moments later a policeman arrived on the scene and asked me if I have something that doesn't belong to me. Then, the earlier bag dropper is supposed to return to the scene and claim to be robbed. I messed-up the scheme. Nobody who sees money in a bag in Russia would return it. I did. I understand that as a part of the scheme the so-called victim claims that there was more money in the bag than was really there, and the victim who wants to stay out of the Russian jails gives extra money to these thieves. Some of these folks have extortion down to a science.

I do want to relay what happened in the safety area in these Russian locations. The plants were extremely unsafe. Incident rates were unacceptably high, including fatalities. The workers wore no safety equipment (hats, glasses, gloves, safety shoes, heat resistant clothing, etc.) Employees without protection were walking over molten metal in the cast house. The cast house roof was leaking and water and molten metal don't mix. This was the worst safety condition I had ever seen.

We decided to make safety a priority. Seven thousand employees were trained in safety in the first year. All employees were given safety equipment and expected to wear it. Compliance was close to 98% in the second month. All departments formed safety committees that met at least monthly. Health and Safety audits were mandatory. We identified fatality risks – and found an astounding 4,000 in the first year. In the first full calendar year that Alcoa owned these facilities (2006) there were no fatalities. Now, these two facilities are approaching six years without a fatality. The incident rates (both Lost Work Days and Total Recordables) are lower than the Alcoa global average (of about 0.10 and 1.00 respectively).

I mention safety because I see safety as an ethical responsibility of the leadership. Sending our employees home in the same condition that they arrived is an ethical responsibility. Identifying risks and eliminating them, providing safety equipment to the workers, training employees on safe work practices are all signs of dignity and respect.

You can imagine that these issues arose regularly. Our employees stole aluminum, ISO Certification was acquired – not earned. I was once robbed by the police – a cop car pulled up to me. Three police got out. They asked for my papers then proceeded to go through my pockets and take $300 and my camera. I recall thinking 'who am I supposed to call?'

Despite these events I still found my three years in Russia to include many, many wonderful experiences. The way the Russians embraced the safety practices was wonderful. The operation becoming profitable was rewarding. I got to meet some wonderful people who are friendly, respectful and love their family and friends. The natural resources in Russia are abundant and beautiful. Given the vast territory, the abundant reserves and the enviable budget surplus in the country, I do believe that with some enlightened leadership Russia could become a true leader among nations and their people will be treated fairly with educational opportunity and the chance to make a difference in their lives and in the world. Pravda!

CHAPTER 8: ETHICS IN PRODUCT DESIGN:

THE CLASH AMONG ENGINEERING, MANAGEMENT, AND PROFITS

--The Ford Pinto: Safety doesn't sell; trunk space does. In 1968 Lee Iacocca, who had introduced the Mustang to much fanfare and applause, recommended to Ford CEO Henry Ford II that the company needed a car to compete in the foreign small-car market, and the Pinto was born. Henry promoted Lee to President, where he flexed his well-known corporate muscle: he wanted the new Pinto in the showrooms by the 1971 model introduction, which meant that the Pinto had to be designed and tooled in record time, violating Habit 8: Consider Time Pressures.

Prior to introduction, Ford engineers conducted crash tests in which eight Pintos were subjected to rear- end collisions. All eight cars with the standard fuel tank failed the tests and were deemed to be potential fire hazards; three were modified successfully. Nevertheless, Ford proceeded to make cars with the standard design in order to meet the introduction date, a price of $2,000, a weight below 2,000 pounds, and ample trunk space. Ford engineers experimented with alternative gas tank locations that met all criteria except ample trunk space. A quote attributed to a Ford engineer was 'safety isn't the issue; trunk space is.' Lee Iacocca was quoted as saying often that 'safety doesn't sell.'

The final review at Ford was a cost/benefit analysis that ascribed a value of $200,725 to a human life. They compared the cost of an $11 gas tank retrofit to the cost of losing an estimated 180 lives and decided that it was three times more expensive to change the standard gas tank design than it was to keep it.

As early as 1973 Ford Field Engineers concluded that the Pinto was susceptible to exploding in low speed (less than 25 mph) rear-end collisions. It was not until 1978 when, faced with litigation over multiple deaths and injuries, public outrage, and government attention that Ford launched a recall of 1.5 million Pintos.

This was less an issue of engineering ethics than it was an issue of arrogance and greed at the top. Engineers designed the car, identified a potential problem and alternative solutions (relocate or retrofit the tank). Their findings were rejected at the top for a number of reasons, including the moldy excuse that 'everyone does it': fuel tanks behind the rear axle were commonplace in American cars at the time. Still, executives decided to proceed knowingly with a hazardous design and an inhuman cost/benefit analysis. When field reports indicated a growing number of fires, Ford did not launch a recall for five more years. Many individuals were in a position to act long before 1978, but they apparently didn't, violating Habit #7 and demonstrating how important corporate culture can be in facing ethical situations objectively.

Lessons learned: I wonder if the engineers and executives at Ford can justify their arrogant pursuit of profits and market share at the expense of lives. I wonder if they can sleep at night; I Know I couldn't if I had been part of this ethical nightmare that actually compared the costs of litigation with the value of human lives.

History tells us that these lessons were learned for more than three decades, during which there is no evidence of similar callousness in the automobile industry. Then, in early 2014, General Motors admitted that faulty ignition switches in 1.6 million small cars had killed at least twelve persons, and that they knew of the danger since 2005, nine years before it became public. Mary Barra, appointed CEO in January of 2014, immediately appointed a safety chief and noted it was only the first of other actions designed to protect the company's reputation for producing safe cars. The jury is still out on what those other actions might be at the time of this writing, when some 20 million vehicles have been recalled.

Then, also in early 2014, Toyota was fined $1.2 billion for deceptive statements made about its problems with sudden acceleration. Although the National Highway Traffic Safety Administration didn't find anything wrong with the vehicles, they found a great deal wrong with the deceit. Honesty pays.

--Mining machinery design: The law of unintended consequences in full bloom. In 1996 the Mine Safety and Health Administration was preparing to publish regulations for approval and use of diesel engines in underground coal mines, including exposure limits for harmful gaseous emissions. At the time, the health effects were not well known, nor were generally accepted limits incorporated in the regulations.

Government scientists measured emissions during tests, and then calculated the amount of fresh air needed to dilute them to a more healthful one milligram per cubic meter. Results were published as part of the process for approving diesel engines. Since all engines were tested in the same manner and emissions diluted to the same level, all manufacturers and mine operators could easily see which engines were dirtiest and cleanest. We expected mine operators to purchase and install the cleanest, and all engine manufacturers to make the cleanest. This expectation was hailed as realistic and fair. Instead, it was naive . Shortly after the test results were published, my associates and I noticed that operators had purchased large numbers of the dirtiest engines, because, lacking emissions controls, they cost less. Regardless of the reasons, that purchasing decision demonstrated a disregard for human health and life and a short-term drive for profits by mine managers. The decisions were legal, but were they ethical? I think not.

Lessons learned: Lower costs for short-term profits trump health and safety, surely an unethical line of reasoning. I'd like to say that the operators were punished in some way other that by their own sense of right, but I can't: They acted within the law, which brings up another terrible lesson: expecting outwardly ethical people to behave ethically at all times is a serious error in judgment; there are too many impediments. And what does this conduct say to engine manufacturers? Will they do the right thing in the future when faced with a similar situation? Or will they focus on lowering costs.

- George Dvorzak, former Engineering Manager, Department of
  Mine Safety, US Department of Mines

CHAPTER 9: ETHICS IN SUPPLIER RELATIONSHIPS:

THE CUSTOMER IS OFTEN OFF-BASE AND CAUGHT STEALING

Blackmail backfires big time: Gorman was a communications manager with a well-deserved reputation for extorting money and other gifts from suppliers, then telling suppliers that they could pay their bills until they were paid back in full. I heard rumors that he had a garage full of gifts ranging from motorcycles to building materials and golf clubs. All, of course, were eventually paid for by his employer's stockholders, and top managers didn't notice or care; I heard rumors that they were 'on the take' as well--isn't it interesting that unethical behavior can become cultural? Most suppliers didn't care either; they enjoyed a steady stream of repeat business based on illegal, unethical actions, or, face it, downright blackmail and extortion openly acknowledged by all parties.

Gorman and I didn't work together often; I think he knew that I wouldn't play his game. But one day he called me and suggested that we meet for lunch at an out-of-the-way restaurant and hinted that he wanted me to write a particularly technical paper for a trade magazine, one of my specialties. I agreed, lunch went well, and I figured I had landed a lucrative and interesting contract.

Then, as we were saying our goodbyes, he suggested that we walk through a nearby boutique known for its magnificent tableware and other home furnishings, all at magnificent prices. As we strolled through the aisles, he pointed out a set of dinnerware and said: 'My wife would love that.' (I often wonder if his wife was in on the scam; I'll never know.)

I got the point, and, as soon as I returned to my office, I called Gorman and told him that I had been given the go-ahead on another project that I had agreed to do months before and, therefore, couldn't accept his kind offer to write his article. I was lying, of course, so in one sense I was behaving unethically by violating Habit #5. In another sense, I was behaving ethically by exchanging my fees for peace of mind and all that entails and not playing his despicable game. So I'm comforted to know that Gorman was behaving unethically and I wasn't.

Gorman called me several times during the ensuing months to offer other assignments, but I was always 'too busy'.

The loser in this case was Gorman, who was forced to work with other writers who did not have the knowledge needed to complete his assignments efficiently. I doubt that he cared.

I was the clear-cut winner: I 'lost' a client that I didn't want or need. How lucky can I get?

Lessons learned: Gorman was in a position of authority in that he had some control over my income, or so he thought. In fact—how could he know?—I had a plethora of respected clients and I have never succumbed to blackmail. So it was easy for me to ignore his authority. I wonder occasionally if he ever realized that. Another lesson: As I mature, I confront unethical behavior directly; I tell the perp that I won't play their game, putting them on notice that their behavior is wrong.

Tell The Truth? Not Me! Roger was the director of communications for a business with sales exceeding five billion dollars per year. He called me in to his office one day to give me a contract to write and visualize a speech concerning a very technical product.

I should have known better than to accept: I had been golfing a week before with one of Roger's direct reports, and, as I was addressing my ball, said to him: 'I'd like to work with Roger.' He raised the universal red warning flag: 'You can't afford to'.

Regardless, I wrote the speech to universal applause, and sent my invoice. A week or so later, Roger called and asked me to meet him in his office. I figured it was to give me more kudos and contracts. He kept me waiting in the lobby for more than an hour, then, when we finally met, he pulled my invoice from his desk drawer, and said: 'It's about your invoice; it's too high.'

I knew it wasn't, and by this time I was fuming. So I grabbed the invoice and tore it up all the while saying:' You didn't have the nerve to tell me, but I know that you had another writer do this job and he couldn't, so his invoice had to be higher than mine since his work was useless, and I know you paid it ...nevertheless ...

'I'll revise my invoice —higher. And I expect to be paid within a week, and if I'm not I'll take the matter up with your boss and tell him how you treat suppliers by wasting their time and coercing them to lower perfectly reasonable invoices'.

I left his office, went back to mine, issued an invoice that was 20 percent higher than the original. He paid it by return mail. I benefitted in two ways by not playing Roger's unethical game: First, I never heard from him again, so I didn't need to think of reasons to not work with him, and, second, I told this story to other communications managers in the company, and their universal response was:

'It's about time somebody told off that crook', and then they awarded me so many new assignments that I could hardly keep up with the work.

Lessons learned: This and the Gorman incident above are similar in that both centered on blackmail by an authority, and I ignored both attempts and profited with peace of mind and cash flow. I think Roger, by never calling me again, got the point—that I reversed our roles and became his ethical authority.

PS: There seems to be constant tension between professional services rendered and their value. For example, as Corporate Patent Counsel I used several outside law firms and often thought their bills were high and unspecific. I questioned the bills periodically, asking for details of work performed. Instead of offering details they issued a lower invoice, which of course made me suspect that they were padding. Therefore, I negotiated fixed fees for certain services, restoring an atmosphere of trust.

CHAPTER 10: ETHICS AND THE LAWYERS:

WHOM CAN YOU TRUST?

Padding invoices and fudging conclusions: Outside experts are retained for their objectivity and independence to complete many tasks in most corporations. Intellectual property infringement is one: A provision in the profession states that intentional infringement of another's valid patent might be penalized with triple damages. One way to avoid that is to retain an independent outside law firm, at a cost of $15,000--$25,000, to provide an opinion that you are not infringing or that the patent is invalid.

When, as Patent Council, I was occasionally faced with this issue I would first draw my own conclusions, and, if I believed we were not infringing, I would still retain an outside law firm to verify it and assure that we would avoid treble damages if a judge or court held differently in the future.

When I sought such advice I would often mask, as much as practicable, who held the patent and who was the alleged infringer, then sent the information to the outside attorney, who would then call me and ask: 'what do you want the opinion to say?' This attorney was prepared to write whatever I wanted; he was willing

to forgo his independence for--what? Money? Repeat business?
I asked this attorney to return my documents, then sent them to a
truly independent and reputable lawyer.

CHAPTER 11: ETHICS IN EMPLOYMENT:

WHY CAN'T WE JUST GET ALONG?

Insider knowledge and the law at war with ethics: My first meeting as Chairman of the Benefits Committee was to handle an appeal by a group of employees protesting a change in severance policy from two to one week's pay for every year of service. The change was made three weeks before a massive layoff.

The financial ramifications were significant for the employees and the company: The average employee would lose $28,000, and the company's cost would be reduced by millions ... an obvious lose-win situation initiated by those who would win.

I learned that the law allowed management to revise certain benefits at any time, without notice, including severance policies. I asked mangers if they knew of the coming layoff when they changed policy, and they admitted that, yes, of course they did, it was the reason the policy was changed. They argued that the current policy was too generous anyway.

My committee operated independently of the company and had a fiduciary responsibility to make its own decisions and recommendations. I informed the President of that business unit that the laid-off employees were entitled to—had a reasonable expectation for-- the larger severance package and the Benefits Committee will grant the employees' appeal--the company must meet its original obligations. After an uncomfortable discussion during which I tactfully pointed out that the President and his staff were behaving unethically, my decision was understood and the original payments reinstated. I know that the President didn't like my decision or me, but I believe I kept his respect.

I believe that the employees were treated fairly and ethically; I hope that the managers involved agree.

Lessons learned: The law and ethics conflict often, and relying on the law to dictate behavior isn't always the right thing to do, even if meeting fiduciary obligations reduces profitability. (APPENDIX B) Also, fiduciary bodies such as a Benefits Committee exist to bring independent judgment to these types of situations. If you serve in this capacity, do so with objectivity and integrity.

Broken promises, broken careers: Gary Forcey, a client and friend, was Marketing Communications Manager at Eaton Corporation for more than 30 years. While at Eaton, he spearheaded a hugely successful marketing campaign to revise every state's building code to require a new circuit breaker that would prevent certain fires and save lives. Revenue and profits more than doubled and Gary was named Marketer of the Year and feted at a banquet attended by hundreds of his peers. His boss was particularly effusive with his praise for a job well done and promised Gary that bigger and better things were in store.

Six weeks later Gary was let go. The same boss who praised his performance and promised a bright future cited the need to reduce costs as the reason. Gary figured the real reason was his age and his relatively high salary that accompanied experience and performance. A week later, his boss hired a younger replacement, presumably at a lower salary.

Justifiably confused and angry, Gary called a law firm to investigate suing for age discrimination. The lawyer said he could, but the case would take years to settle, the outcome was uncertain, and the costs would be several thousands. Gary decided to move on. Unable to find a job in communications—he figured because of his age--he tried selling advertising and cars but wasn't challenged. He eventually went to work at an industrial market research firm as a telephone interviewer at about one-third his previous income.

David Zimomra's career has followed a similar pattern. While employed as a senior vice president at a large engineering firm, he was lauded by his superiors for his obvious abilities to book new business. He was told by the owners that he was being groomed to be CEO within a year. A month or so later he was fired for reasons that he still does not understand and his former employer refuses to discuss. Like Gary, he investigated suing but decided it was too costly and traumatic.

David worked as a consultant, then as an employee, and then as a consultant again. His income is less than half of what it was while employed, and his life is more unsettled. He is still disillusioned that anybody would so blatantly lie to him.

Lessons learned: In both cases the bosses violated Habit #5, tell the truth, the whole truth, and nothing but the truth. I wonder if mendacity is at the root of most—perhaps all? – ethical lapses.

CHAPTER 12: ETHICS IN ENVIRONMENTAL COMPLIANCE:

TRUST IS THE HEART OF CONSTRUCTIVE RELATIONSHIPS

Act now, ask permission later: Late one afternoon, when I was in charge of the environmental area for Alcoa, an environmental engineer called to tell me that the groundwater adjacent to one plant contained trichloroethylene (TCE).

I had many more questions than facts: Why take the sample? (we had a consent decree with the state that required the company to take groundwater samples adjacent to all plants every three years); When was the contaminated sample taken? (today). Do we own the plant? (yes, it was included in a major acquisition of 80 plants. It is now closed and hasn't operated for more than four years..) Did the TCE definitely come from our operations? (uncertain, but it might have.) How harmful is TCE? (unknown, but surely a carcinogen if ingested.) Are people ingesting it? (yes, the 125 families in the city drink well water from the same aquifer); Have you reported the results to the state? (not yet, but we must do so within 90 days) At the time, Alcoa's vision was to be the best company in the world, with one part of 'best' to be the most socially responsible and the model in community relations; we aspired to be a good neighbor. We knew we had a way to go if we were to meet that ideal. I reminded my direct reports of our vision, and asked 'how would the best company in the world behave if confronted with this situation?' Also, what behavior would be expected if your family lived in this city?

I called our company's lawyer and asked him how I should act: 'Do nothing; if you do anything, you might be seen as admitting liability.' That's surely not how the best company in the world would behave, so my direct reports and I considered that advice as unwise, rejected it, and came up with a better plan.

At 8AM the next day our engineers in the state advised all 125 families in the area and local government officials of the sample results, gave all families a week's supply of bottled water, and promised to replenish the supply for at least two to three weeks while we installed new filters on their wells—a decision that cost Alcoa about one million dollars. We decided to act quickly and without asking permission of our top executives (I knew that the CEO would approve, and we'd sort out any legal liability later. He had clearly set and communicated the tone and expectations that the company would do what's right.)

I often ask my business school students what they think of our decision, and how they think shareholders might react. Most disapproved, opining that shareholders' interests are strictly financial. I then point out that, yes, while shareholders are interested in financial results, they are also interested in the sustainability of the firm, and behaving in the interests of all stakeholders, including the communities in which the business operates, is one key to sustain-ability. I suggest that 80 percent of shareholders would approve. Besides, I ask in somewhat of a coup de grace, how do you know that the cost of future liabilities of doing nothing would be less than the current liabilities of acting immediately? In my experience, doing what's right and doing it quickly is always less expensive than delay, obstruction, or concealment.

Lessons learned: Don't compromise your principles, in this case the company's vision, which is related to Habit # 4: Interpret the rules objectively; bend them prudently. Also, imagine yourself and your family in the same situation; it will help you to see what is right.

CHAPTER 13: ETHICS IN COMMUNICATIONS:

REPRESSING OR BROADCASTING INFORMATION CAN CREATE ETHICAL ISSUES

The compliance hotline: Truth, rumor, or revenge? When I was the Vice President for Corporate Environment, Health, and Safety--where the buck stops when it comes to monitoring all aspects of Alcoa's safety --I received an anonymous report from Australia on the ethics hotline: 'Our plant manager is suppressing information regarding industrial accidents.' That's it. I was charged with investigating and resolving this issue, and will demonstrate how by applying the six-steps to ethical power:

First, I recognized a potential ethical issue: Investigating tips of this sort is required by law and corporate policy--Alcoa investigates all reports on the ethics hotline-- as well as common sense. As with many complex, difficult matters, many issues need to be addressed beyond economics or liabilities. A cover-up, masking, hiding or manipulation of the truth raises an ethical issue that I could ignore only if I wanted to put my career and my organization on the line.

Sharing of such information with others could actually prevent a similar incident from occurring at another location, preventing an injury to another person. So, suppressing such information could actually result in injuries to others that could be avoided.

Second, I researched the facts. Allegations are easy, especially anonymously; verifying them isn't. In this case, I delegated the task of researching facts to a trusted associate with a strong reputation for integrity and safety record-keeping. I sent her to the plant to review records and reports and to interview employees. Her conclusion verified that the allegation was indeed accurate: approximately 50 incidents had not been reported, 90% of which were relatively minor medical treatment situations.

Her interviews also verified that the Plant Manager was encouraging employees and the Safety Manager not to report these incidents. She also found that the Plant Manager was performing very well in operations, sales, inventory reduction, quality, and employee engagement. The Plant Manager was on a career path and was being groomed to succeed his boss in the next six months. There were no other allegations or issues regarding his behavior or performance.

Third, I reposed to uncover my options: Was the Plant Manager the sole offender? Were there co-conspirators? Answering these questions is also a part of a thorough investigation. The Plant Manager's boss, whose office was thousands of miles away, was a very strong supporter and champion for workplace safety, so he was excluded from my list of possible co-conspirators. Therefore, I decided that the Plant Manager was accountable and responsible, which can be a tricky decision. For example, bosses and officers, often driven, charismatic leaders, might push for better and better results and might tell others that they don't want to read about safety incidents, which could be construed as condoning unethical behavior, and subordinates might bow to their authority.

Is such a statement a suggestion to subordinates that the truth should not be reported? Should the reality of the situation be suppressed? Of course not.

Fourth, I reconciled the options: I confronted the accused party or parties with the allegation and the factual summary of the investigation, and asked for their reaction. At this stage additional facts are often uncovered that might warrant additional investigation. Sometimes additional information about the state of mind, health concerns or personal pressures on the accused party or parties may surface that may or may not be relevant to the situation. In this particular case, the accused Plant Manager denied the allegation, but could not refute the facts uncovered in the investigation. The accused stated that he never actually instructed his employees not to report safety incidents, but he may have overly stressed the importance of a clean safety record.

119

Once the facts have been verified and the accused has had an opportunity to tell his side of the story, there are usually a few options regarding acting to punish the behavior or not, to investigate further or not, to publicize the situation or not, and to educate the organization on proper behavior and ethical expectations or to forget the incident

One option, of course, was to do nothing, which is fair if the facts exonerate the accused by being false or inconclusive. Another option is to investigate further, which can help to prevent similar behavior is elsewhere in the organization. On the other hand, resolving one issue without examining, at least cursorily, to determine if similar issues exist elsewhere sends a message that the behavior is only wrong when you get caught, or when it is reported.

Five, I responded: Depending on what one uncovers, unethical behavior may deserve to be punished by mild reprimand, a minor penalty such as being passed over for a raise, a major penalty such as being passed over for a promotion, or the more major penalty of being fired. In this case, others decided that the Plant Manager had already fired himself, and he was let go. We decided to explain the situation to other Plant Managers throughout the company, knowing full well that tens of thousands of employees were watching and the rumor mill was functioning as efficiently as ever.

Six, we reviewed: I asked myself and the associate that I sent to the plant all the questions posed in CHAPTER 3, Step 6. Our answers revealed that we acted appropriately with one exception: we wondered if our choice of punishment was too harsh, and we should have merely reprimanded the Plant Manager to tell our employees that we are a compassionate employer. We decided that in this case the punishment was appropriate since a corporate value had been breached.

Lessons Learned: The six-step procedure works to arrive at objective, realistic resolutions of ethical issues of all types; it works for me, and it can work for all readers. Punishing ethical violations is an opportunity to reinforce the values and expectation to the organization. On the other hand, not punishing can be seen as hypocrisy at the top.

Airport eavesdropping: Are public conversations public knowledge? Part I: I was in the airport lounge when I overheard four buyers from a large customer discussing, in detail, upcoming contract negotiations with my employer. Although I wasn't directly involved, I did know the managers who were.

First, I immediately recognized an ethical issue: I knew right away that I faced an ethical issue: I could clearly hear every word of a conversation that involved strategic and confidential information. Although these buyers should have no expectation of privacy in a public place, and it is not illegal for me to listen, listening seemed wrong and unfair.

Second, I researched the facts in a few minutes: My thoughts proceeded along these lines: We live in a world in which we fight for competitive advantage; therefore I see nothing unethical about listening to this conversation, and I felt obligated to take the information being carelessly shared and then quickly communicate it to the appropriate managers who could use it, which might enhance my reputation and advance my career. On top of that, the conversers were in a public place and should not expect privacy.

In fact, it could be rationalized that these individuals are at fault for their own stupidity for discussing intimate negotiation details in a public place. Clearly, there is nothing illegal about listening to others talk in a public place where there are no expectations of privacy. But should a determination of legality orient one's ethical compass?

Third, I reposed: I had very little time to deliberate. I needed to act, but how? Doing nothing would allow the situation to continue and intensify; it is not an option. I could leave the area or put ear phones in my ears and not listen, or I could warn the conversers and ask them to talk about other things.

Fourth, I reconciled my options, and decided that the two that prevented my hearing any more of the conversation were equally acceptable. But I could also choose to inform them of what they were doing.

Fifth, I responded: I stood, turned around, and faced group. I told them who I was and where I worked. I shook their hands. They continued to talk, and I asked myself: Now what--was informing them enough to relieve me of any further ethical obligation? Am I still required to walk away? What would you do? I'll argue that informing was good ethical behavior and that walking away would also be prudent ethical behavior. We all have a moral compass, and hope that it points to what is right. In this case, I sat, listened, took notes and called my friend--the involved marketing manager who would meet with these folks the next day, and told him what happened. The marketing manager asked if I told them who I was, a question that reflects the ethical culture in Alcoa at the time--and that he would be uncomfortable with any information that was obtained unfairly.

Sixth, I reviewed: I spread this story throughout Alcoa to alert employees of the need to protect company information, to be careful of conversations in public places.

Lessons Learned: Interpret the rules objectively and bend them prudently. It's Habit #4 in CHAPTER 4, and adhering to it is a sure way to enhance your reputation. And follow your moral compass; doing so will usually lead you to doing what is right.

Airplane eavesdropping: Are public conversations public knowledge? Part II: I was flying back to my office after a long and fruitful meeting concerning a large engineering/construction contract with a major customer when I heard my competitor discuss the same contract in the seats behind me. I was young and ambitious—my lame excuse for my subsequent behavior--so I tuned in, thinking that I would gain competitive advantage and be rewarded with huge accolades from my boss, Jim Sharpe, who I discuss briefly in CHAPTER 19.

I excitedly took mental and written notes and looked forward to spilling the beans to Jim and others the next morning. I never thought for a second that I was acting unethically; I was in a competitive game and needed all the help I could muster to win contracts and promotions. I presented my findings to Jim and his boss, and was met with extreme indifference. The information would not change our proposal one bit, which was our best and final offer and let the chips fall where they may.

Lessons learned: Ambition, a form of arrogance, can lead to

unethical behavior; be humble. Stop and pause periodically to be sure your ethical filter is working. Then be comfortable with doing what's right.

PS: You may relate to these similar situations: A person leaves his briefcase in your office after a meeting. Can you look inside and read the notes? Of course not. But what if he discarded his notes in a waste basket? Can you retrieve them? What if a competitor sends you cost or other information by mistake? Can you use the information to create a competitive advantage? By anticipating these and similar situations you will be more habitually inclined to do what's right when the real situation takes place.

CHAPTER 14: ETHICS BEYOND THE LAW:

HOW TO LOSE FRIENDS AND ALIENATE PEOPLE

My ethical compass went berserk: The players: Sally, CEO and the sole investor in Gizmo, a long-time friend who has said often that 'You are the brother I never had'; and Tom, President of Gizmo, a lawyer/politician who somehow convinced Sally to invest more than $1M (estimates vary between 1.3 and 3.0M) in Gizmo, most or all of which Sally borrowed.

The issue: My $1500 invoice for writing Gizmo's website and meeting with a designer.

Sally burst into my home at 7AM, carrying her coffee pot, and, before even saying 'good morning', said: 'We won't pay your invoice for writing our website. Tom asked me to tell you because you and I are such good friends.'

'Why won't you pay me?' I asked. 'The invoice is four, five months old and neither you nor Tom has told me that it is unfair.'

'Because we can't use what you wrote.'

'Why,' I asked again. 'Tom was totally satisfied with it when he reviewed it with me right here on my dining room table. He even said that it is exactly what he needed and wanted; very complimentary.'

Step 1. Recognize: I sensed an ethical issue in the making, and knew I faced a legal issue of not paying a legitimate invoice. Is a legal issue automatically and ethical issue?

Sally: 'The person who was to design the site for a small fee didn't know how, so we fired him, and we can't afford a professional designer. We're talking to a student who may do it for nothing. So we can't use what you wrote.'

Step 2: Research, in this case the twisted 'facts'.

'Not my problem. Totally irrelevant to my work.'

Step 3: Repose: At this point I knew I faced a logic disconnect, a false and self-serving rationalization and I started to become angry and struggled to hide it.

Sally: 'We overpaid your son for the photos for the website, and I gave him two hours of free advice on the drive to and from the plant.'

Me: 'Still not germane to my work. I suggest that you talk to him about those issues. He's 43 and able to handle his own affairs. Or, if you want, deduct $500 from my invoice and pay me the balance. Besides, although it's irrelevant, I charged you one-third of my normal fee for this kind of work simply because you're my friend. And you volunteered to advise my son; he didn't ask for it; you could have talked about the Steelers.'

Sally: 'Still can't pay you . . . we're in a cash bind and aren't paying our suppliers. You can sue us if you want, but you'll have to get in line.'

Me: 'Still not my problem. If you couldn't pay, you should not have hired me.'

Sally: 'Besides, you don't need the money; you have plenty.'

Me: 'Still not relevant. I don't work for nothing and neither do you. Let's apply your thinking to you: You claim to be worth nine million, which I assure you is far more than I'm worth, and you have a million in your pension plan, and I'm betting you still expect to be paid for your work. Besides, you have no idea of my finances, so you're guessing.'

Epilogue: During the 6+months that have elapsed since the above scene played out, Sally has purchased a new Lincoln - $50K? - demonstrating that she thinks more highly of her car than she does of me.

Sally does not come to my home for her usual Thursday coffee visits and has not invited my lady friend that she describes as her 'sister' and me to any of her frequent parties.

THE BOTTOM LINE: Sally and Tom have behaved illegally (breach of contract); unethically (not paying me for reasons that are irrelevant and self-serving), and disrespectfully (my talent is valueless for irrelevant reasons)… three ethical strikes.

THE BIG QUESTIION: Did they think that there would be no consequences of their actions? Did they really think that I would accept their behavior unconditionally? Is that the epitome of arrogance? (Yes, in my view.)

Step 4: Review my options.

OPTION 1: Report this to the Better Business Bureau to warn other suppliers that they won't be paid. If I do, will I help to bankrupt Gizmo and put its 30 or so employees out of work? This option turned out to be irrelevant: Gizmo filed for CHAPTER 11 bankruptcy shortly after the incident in my home. The firm is being liquidated.

OPTION 2: Walk away and hope that I never see Sally or Tom again, which is unlikely given the proximity of our homes. Rejected as unrealistic.

OPTION 3: Behave as if nothing happened, aka total forgiveness and a return to the previous rounds of parties and coffee breaks, which is unacceptable to my desire to associate with people I can trust.

OPTION 4: Be cordial when we come across each other and avoid closer social contact.

Step 5: ACT

Accept option #4.

Step 6: REVIEW

I limit contact with Sally to the occasional 'hello' as we cross paths in our neighborhood. We are cordial and she is cordial toward me. I actually feel sorry for her.

How Sally and Tom could have behaved: 1. Explain their cash problem and ask me to wait a few months for payment and I would have gladly agreed. 2. Loan the firm $1500 from their personal funds and pay me without comment. 3. Pay me directly from their personal account and invoice the firm. 4. Pay me a nominal sum per month, say $50.

How I could have behaved: I could have filed a lawsuit to collect the money owed and I'm sure secure a judgment, but that would merely put me in a long line of other creditors and waste time.

Lessons Learned: Perhaps it isn't wise to do business with family and friends; it's too easy for disputes to fester. Clarify business matters before doing the work, and terminate work at the first sign of tension to preserve wanted relationships. And, finally, if you promise to pay, do so and create trust, a basis for all constructive human relationships.

CHAPTER 15: GIFTS AND BRIBERY:

THE FINE LINE

Can friendship and business live happily ever after? Gifting persists everywhere in most firms, which can lead to ethical issues and the need for greater awareness and guidelines. Most procurement and sales organizations--where gifting is most prevalent--do a very good job of educating their buyers and sales professionals about the policy on giving and receiving gifts. However, those employees, even those who are more ethically mature, are often unaware that ethical issues could be involved.

I recall when Alcoa had a corporate Medical Director, an MD, who reported to me. He returned from his honeymoon and told me that two of his doctor friends, who also happened to be medical consultants to Alcoa, came to his wedding and presented him with cash gifts of $2,000 each. I explained to him that some people might interpret this as him inviting his suppliers to his wedding in exchange for kickbacks. He said that's not what happened, these folks are friends, they gave him those gifts out of the goodness of their hearts. After an hour of discussion, he agreed to return the money.

Lesson Learned: This situation could have and should have been avoided. He could invite them but write on the invitation 'given our business relationship, gifts would be inappropriate. I hope you can attend the wedding.' Another lesson learned: Even highly intelligent and educated people who should know better often do not recognize ethical dilemmas. Still another: Trust your instincts; if it feels or appears wrong, don't do it.

CHAPTER 16: ETHICS IN SPORTS: WHAT ARE WE TEACHING?

THE GOOD, THE BAD, THE UGLY

What's the upside? The downside? : Sports can be wonderful, real-world experiences that teach valuable lifelong lessons. Early in life, sports teach children dexterity, coordination, physical and mental fitness, teamwork, and leadership. Players learn to follow and respect the rules set by the game, coaches, and officials, and expect all players to do the same, demonstrating fairness and honesty. And they learn that hard work is usually rewarded by a win with which they can be justifiably proud.

In short, sports early in life and the coaches and officials--often volunteers--can lay the groundwork for adults to live ethically. However, there are downsides as well. Sports open opportunities to cheat, for example use of ineligible players, and to bully less talented players, displaying intolerance. When winning is given extraordinary importance, developing talent and character tend to be ignored ... literally destroying the main purpose of sports. Coaches who behave in that manner send the wrong message and, in yet another example of tone being set at the top, it will be absorbed by players, endangering the ethical society we want. The parallels with business are clear: The executive who wants to win at any cost is the executive who is tempted to behave unethically to do so. This book is riddled with examples. In contrast, the executive who prizes development of talent and character, who doesn't compromise the sound principles of ethical behavior, will be rewarded over the long haul, as will his organization.

That said, I am sickened by the mayhem that is allowed in sports arenas and glorified by the media that would be criminal offenses if committed anywhere else. For example, a hockey player was attacked--the acceptable euphemism is 'checked'--from his blind side, then punched unconscious while lying prone on the ice and then wheeled from the arena on a gurney. The perpetrator skated off the ice into the dressing room before he could be penalized. His victim suffered a concussion and was hospitalized for several days and could not play for a week; the perp was suspended for five games, hardly a slap on the wrist for such gratuitous brutality.

If that had happened outside the arena, the perp would have been charged with assault and battery, perhaps attempted murder. Amazingly, the victim forgave the perp, saying in essence that these things happen in the heat of the game. I can be excused for thinking that he was protecting his own future, hoping that he would be given the same slap on the wrist should he behave in the same way.

This was only one of three major fights that broke out during that one game; think of the hundreds that broke out in other games around the world.

Hockey seems to be a hot bed of such thuggery-- except in the Olympics, where speed and finesse are still prized-- but other sports are in the same smarmy boat. Where are the leaders? Their actions, or their lack of actions, are setting the tone.

I, for one, will not attend or view hockey games, in part because I feel that the special lenient treatment given to athletes is amoral, not only in the arena, but also outside.

I also predict that mayhem in the arena will diminish as soon as our plethora of lawyers recognize that it is a huge and untapped market for lawsuits and convince victims to sue.

Equal justice for all? Don't bet on it. And, BTW, the Associated Press named, in late December, the Boston Marathon bombing as the sports story of 2012, effectively calling a bombing a sport. Universities justify their huge sports programs by avowing that sports are part of a well-rounded education that builds character, strong values, and a greater sense of ethics. Yet, as Rushmore Kidder reports in his book, How Good People Make Tough Choices: "Intercollegiate sports, as currently played on the competitive, televised, and money-sodden fields of many of today's campuses, apparently does just the reverse. It takes whatever capacity for moral reasoning the athletes bring with them and corrodes it slowly away as the seasons pass."

I'm reminded of Peter Drucker's comment that when an institution loses its focus on its primary goal, it is on the road to oblivion. Perhaps universities and professional sports might heed the warning.

They might also consider that they too often live, clearly and vividly, the definition of unethical that I love so much—the disconnect between words and actions. Examples abound, but one stands out. Early in 2008, the owner of a professional football team announced that he was getting out of the business of rehabilitating the ten players on his ream who had been arrested during the previous fourteen months. Included among the ten was a wide receiver who had been arrested five times. The owner stated clearly that this player's conduct can no longer be tolerated, echoing a local judge who called the player a one-man crime wave.

Nevertheless, and in a remarkable and shameful display of self-interest overcoming any sense of honesty and ethics, the owner gave the player one more chance and a two-year contract worth multi-millions just four months after he was released by the team. The unstated reason: injuries to two other players, requiring a quick fix despite being so obviously unethical and self-serving — at least to me, but I wonder about the team's fans.

Unethical behavior in sports, in my view, is of epidemic proportions and expanding as we speak, perhaps because we value winning at all costs. The Spygate scandal, where the coach of the New England Patriots was caught stealing signals of rival teams , led to the largest fine--$500,000--ever imposed by the National Football League. Perhaps not so strangely, a retired coach of another team said on TV that 'everyone does it; he (the Patriot's coach) got caught'. 'Everyone does it' is not an excuse for unethical behavior; it smacks of the Nuremburg Trials and is sure to trigger an avalanche of similar behavior, just what we don't want in a civil society. I hope that the NFL is now investigating all teams.

I could continue, starting with players who take performance-enhancing drugs and accept expensive gifts , and coaches who break contracts to accept what they perceive to be a 'better' job. Nevertheless, in all fairness, some professional sports are addressing the ethics of their sport. The NFL, for example, has new rules of contact designed to prevent injuries, particularly concussions. And Major League Baseball has new rules designed to prevent injuries caused by runners colliding with catchers as they slide into home plate. I see these and other moves to protect players from injury as akin to Alcoa's tremendously successful focus on safety, as described so vividly in CHAPTER 7 and elsewhere in this book.

CHAPTER 17: ETHCS IN QUALITYASURANCE (QA):

HOW FAR CAN THE RULES BE BENT?

Lying and bypassing corporate values. An Operations Superintendent shipped product without inspecting for quality as required by the customer. After a thorough investigation by my delegate, I was told that the QA equipment broke and product was shipped in order to meet monthly sales targets. The superintendent admitted that his decision was unilateral, and justified it by noting that no defects had been uncovered for the past month so he assumed-- by a strange leap of logic--that the product was fine. He was proud to have met sales goals, and I was faced with an ethical dilemma. I examined my options.

1. Do nothing: Sometimes an initial investigation exonerates the accused, or the evidence is insufficient to draw a conclusion. Ergo, not acting is a fair response. Nevertheless, there is value in communicating to the organization that the situation was investigated and the rationale for the conclusion. But, when unethical behavior is found action is necessary to either confirm or refute the behavior, and the action must be ASAP; delay will be seen as indecision and/or confusion.

2. Reprimand: I rejected this slap on the wrist as being far too lenient. Before doing so, however, I considered the message that I would send to others: I don't take ethical violations seriously, cronyism is rampant at the higher levels of management, the punishment is laughable, and so on, all detrimental to the culture that we had spent years to create but that can be destroyed overnight.

3. Terminate: Unethical behavior deserves to be punished in ways that fit the behavior---most often a difficult decision. When federal judges are asked 'What is the most difficult part of your job?', they typically reply 'sentencing', even if there are sentencing guidelines. Corporations do not have guidelines except for a few situations, so managers face an even more difficult task, and sentencing can be based on such intangibles as prior behavior, sincere remorse, intent or its lack, and damage. When the core values of the organization have been violated, there is likely less room for forgiveness.

In this case, a contractual commitment was intentionally broken--a breach of legal as well as ethical obligations and expectations. The customer was immediately notified of the breach, and the Superintendent was fired.

Lessons learned: The Superintendent interpreted the rules to enhance his operations and financial performance, surely not prudent in an organization dedicated to quality as one cause of sustainability. Arrogance also entered the picture; I am certain that he never thought he'd be caught, or, even if he was, he would be forgiven. The situation also raises doubt about the ethical tone set by leaders; obviously it was not well-established or communicated, opening opportunities to do so.

A quality control (QC) engineer goes rogue: Truth or an angry whistle-blower? The non-descript voice on the corporate compliance line left a cryptic message, one of 1200/year at Alcoa: 'The QC engineer is approving product that hasn't been inspected.' My first reaction was that some angry whistle-blower with a grudge against the QC engineer, who I knew and respected, was on a vendetta, and I should discount the message. Then I thought: 'What if it's true? What if the QC engineer really was bending the rules? It's happened before. And besides, isn't the caller behaving unethically by hiding his identity? Does he know that we have rules that protect whistle blowers from retaliation?

When the whistle blows it must be heard and an intervention must be conducted. If not, the compliance line becomes a sham. My gut told me to investigate thoroughly, that this was a potential ethical issue that could have severe consequences on the finances and reputation of the company and me personally. So I visited the plant and reviewed the QA and maintenance repair reports and found a glaring conflict: the QA reports continued to show stellar results while the test equipment was being repaired, obviously impossible.

When confronted, the QC engineer explained that he didn't want to interrupt shipments and cash flow, that he thought the plant manager would agree although the two didn't discuss the matter, and, besides, the product would be used in window frames, not a critical application such as airplane parts.

I pointed out that the company leaned on its reputation for quality for its sustainability, its long-term viability. The company has integrity, and if our contact with the customer specified inspection, we inspect; our values cannot be compromised for any reason. The QC engineer was replaced.

I never tried to learn who left the message; it isn't important. What is important is that this person saw an ethical issue and decided to not bend the rules. Did he ignore authority? I'll never know. Perhaps he was the authority himself, although I doubt it.

Lessons learned: Adhering to steps 1 and 2 in the process for ethical behavior-- recognize and research—led to thwarting an ethical issue before it eroded the company's cash flow and reputation.

CHAPTER 18: ETHICS IN FINANCIAL MANAGEMENT:

CONFLICTS OF INTEREST AND OTHER AVOIDABLE DILEMMAS

Recognizing them can be tough, resolving them tougher. I feel that many ethical issues arise from conflicts of interest, as some of the anecdotes in this book demonstrate. I was particularly enlightened by the QA engineer in Chapter I7 who was torn between meeting short-term sales goals and long-term testing requirements, and he erroneously chose the short term and was fired. I ran into a similar situation during the early stages of my career in finance.

Before we formed Allegheny Financial I was in trained for a few weeks by a middle-aged gentleman who impressed me with his intelligence and articulation. We spent considerable time on a particular product that he was pushing to the point of hype. New to the industry and the business, I presented it to customers, and, to my surprise, sold it despite feeling that it was more fluff that substance. To this day, almost 40 years later, I am disappointed that I sold it once, but am pleased to say that I never sold another. Within three years I left that company, started Allegheny with a partner--in part because I could set my own ethical standards--and moved on.

About 15 years ago, a client, a very respected executive as well as a one-third owner of a very successful company, was discussing his company. Three people owned this company, and one worked as the president. I had looked closely at the organizational and financial structure; it required double taxation, first by the corporation and again by the shareholders.

Many years before this the IRS had changed the rules to eliminate this wasteful and expensive--to earners-- practice. Their advisor/accountant was older, a former IRS agent, and probably too busy to be current with tax changes. He adamantly vetoed my proposal for an alternative tax structure. I did not have the verbal skills to overcome the strained logic of why it was not a beneficial move. I always thought he was too embarrassed to admit to his ignorance, but my client knew I was correct. Sometime in the next ten years I ran into one of the other principals who, to my surprise, commented, out of nowhere, 'You know you were correct about that tax change.' That emotional issue cost hundreds of thousands of dollars for the group, and I still think of that former IRS agent as unethical.

Have you ever noticed that business persons will often talk about IRS agents as not the sharpest knives in the drawer? However when a business person's accountant/advisor is an 'ex-IRS agent' he or she suddenly gains an aura of great respect and (insider) knowledge. I really believe many IRS agents are very competent. A few, as in any other profession, aren't.

Discussing a competitor with a prospective client is always an ethical challenge. If it's a competitor I don't know, I just listen, question why they are talking to me, and often stress our service, which I am convinced is exceptional. If it is a competitor I know and respect, I tell the person accordingly and might say that they may not be getting bad advice from my competitor, but they would probably get better service from me. If it is a competitor I know and respect and think of as a friend, I would rather the person not change unless there is a real chemistry issue. If it is a competitor I know, and know their specific recommendations aren't appropriate, I feel it my ethical duty to tell the prospective client that and in fact comment that they should leave that advisor whether they are going to us or another advisor.

I have never worked for a large house, the Merrill Lynch's of the world, but I have hired individuals from those firms. Two issues jump out at me concerning their business models and conflicts of interest. One had, and maybe others as well, a minimum revenue requirement to remain at the firm. This is reviewed quarterly for new employees. With that onus/pressure on a new employee, it can become very difficult for that person to think more about the best interests of the client and less about commissions. In addition, this training philosophy affects behavior well into the future.

Another firm told employees that the employee would not be paid commissions on any client with assets less than $250,000. Simply put, the firm would keep those revenues. Again, what kind of an impact on a supposed culture of service would that have?

A culture can be built within a company that creates an expectation of behavior and service. Any behavior by any employee outside this range is quickly known by all, and explanations need to be forthcoming. Obviously, rules and guidelines need to match this expected behavior.

- Jim Browne, Founding Partner, Allegheny Financial Group

CHAPTER 19: ETHICS IN THE BOARDROOM:

CRONYISM AND BIAS RUN AMOK

The rubber-stamp syndrome: Directors owe a fiduciary responsibility to shareholders to adequately monitor their company's officers, especially as regards to unethical and/or illegal conduct. In too many cases, they fail to meet that responsibility, which can be demonstrated by answers to the following queries: Would directors have approved of Dennis Kozlowski's $6000 shower curtain, $15,000 umbrella stand, and $2 million birthday party for his wife, all paid for by stockholders, if they were meeting their responsibilities? Would ENRON and Arthur Anderson have collapsed if the directors had known about the Ponzi scheme and the accounting manipulations? Would Westinghouse have been bankrupted if directors had known about management's reckless investments in real estate, a business in which the company had little or no expertise? The answer to these and countless other similar questions concerning destructive and self-serving behavior by top executives is a resounding 'of course not', but only if you believe that directors:

• are on top of day-to-day operations and strategies--they aren't and can't be; they have other lives, often as top executives in another firm or as consultants. They meet typically for a day once every three months, largely to approve quarterly financial statements that officers have organized to paint their performance in the brightest light possible, of course using generally accept able accounting procedures and complying with all regulations of the SEC, FCPA, Sarbanes Oxley and others. Therefore, it is difficult or impossible for them to know and understand operations except in the very broadest, most abstract sense. In addition, officers set the agendas for board meetings and board committee meetings and control the information presented, as well as the presenters.

• behave in ways that benefit the long-term viability of the company and its stakeholders; and
• aren't indebted in some way to top officers but rather are truly independent.

The bottom line is that directors face a major ethical issue: Many are paid outlandish sums (hundreds of thousands of dollars per year at the major public corporations) to perform an impossible task: monitor the behavior of and advise officers without the close perspective of the officers themselves. Directors are, for the most part, making decisions based, at times, on incomplete and biased information.

A caveat: I've known a few truly conscientious and ethical

149

directors who do not fit the profile I've painted in the above bullets. I've also known others --surely the majority in my circle--who condone five or more years of corporate losses, rationalize a lack of corporate strategy/direction, forgive repeated legal fines under the same leadership, and somehow explain away a disgraceful record of exploiting the environment. I wonder how they look themselves in the mirror or how peacefully they sleep.

My feelings about directors were confirmed when I read this short quote in the Pittsburgh Tribune Review of February 9, 2014: 'The board has been absent without leave for the last several years when this company (US Steel) has fallen into great difficulty.' The quote is from Charles Bradford, a steel industry analyst, about a proposal to increase accountability of the board.

CHAPTER 20: THE AUTHORS BARE THEIR SOULS IN A CONVERSATIONAL SMMARY:

A CONVERSATIONAL SUMMARY

Pete: The anecdotes we've told are only a small cross section of our experiences with ethical and unethical issues; we've witnessed and lived many more. For example, I've been duped out of serious money at least twice by friends who are no longer my friends. In one case, a friend who happened to be my mentor when I first worked as a sales engineer, pleaded that he needed $10, 000 to pay the health insurance premiums for his employees and promised with heartfelt sincerity that he would pay me back in a week. I still have his IOU in my desk drawer some 20 years later, and when I accidently see him on the streets he insists that I will get my money 'soon'. I wrote off the 10k years ago and feel sorry that he is so deluded and unethical.

Bill: Loan money to a friend and lose the friend and the money. Is that any different than mishandling company funds for self-serving purposes? I think not.

Pete: I agree. The General Manager of a large business unit hired me to write a short presentation to the board explaining why the entire business--including building a new plant to replace an oldie but goodie-- had to move from Philadelphia to Orlando, Florida.

His main reason: His engineers needed to be closer to a major university and its research scientists and library—as if Philadelphia doesn't have major universities. Turns out he was a few years from retirement and wanted the company to pay to move him and his yacht to a warmer clime. Believe it or not, the board approved the move, proving once again that boards often are rubber stamps, which is unethical in itself. The cost to stockholders had to be many millions. Was I unethical for writing his gangbusters presentation and being part of a sham?

Bill: I can answer that with either a yes or no. Regardless, I experienced a similar incident when a top exec wanted one of his direct reports to justify housing a company plane at an airport close to his home. The direct report tried three times before his boss was satisfied with the rationale, which of course was a bunch of self-serving hooey that any astute person could see.

Pete: Bill, we've mentioned several times in this book that ethical people bend the rules only if absolutely necessary, that they adhere to their principles no matter the circumstances. I worked for many years at Dravo Corporation, where my direct boss was Jim Sharpe, a brilliant engineer and businessman who never bent the rules until he bowed to authority, which we discussed earlier as something to avoid if you want to encourage ethical behavior.

The board hired a financial guy to be President, the first who wasn't an engineer and long-time employee. This newbie was charged by the board to raise the price of the company's stock, and he set stretch goals that were difficult or impossible to meet. Jim compromised his principles and booked several huge contracts at below-cost prices, hoping to make up the difference with extra work. It didn't happen, and Jim was fired and, soon after, the company went bankrupt. Who behaved unethically?

Bill: Along the same lines--and as I discussed in CHAPTER 7--I was transferred by Alcoa to Russia to manage two enormous plants with more than 15,000 employees. I brought 68 ex-pats from eight different countries with me. Before going, I made a conscious decision that I would instill Alcoa's values and mission into all operations and my actions. I started my tenure there by insisting on open offices to encourage communications, and training all employees about the importance of safety in the plants, and I rejected all attempts at bribery and corruption. Those decisions created some serious problems at times. For example, I was detained in a back room of an airport and was told I would be freed if I paid a few thousand rubles, and was even told I could be escorted to an ATM. I refused, and once I was let go after nine hours.

Pete: I've always disagreed with the common belief that ethical is what you are when nobody is looking. It's trite, attributed to coaches, motivational speakers, and fortune cookie writers. Still. Its popularity demonstrates the power behind it. Ethics is what you do when your conscience is looking, and your conscience is always looking. That's another way of saying that ethical behavior is a full-time job.

Bill: These days, more than your conscience is always looking at your behavior; the social media are looking at you all the time and creating a permanent record. If Anthony Wiener, for example, had used his phone as a phone instead of a peep hole into his question-able ethics, he might have become Mayor of New York.
Some business persons don't get the notion that ethics is a full-time job. For example, I was asked by a CEO of a mid-size manufacturer to visit and tell him about ethics and its need. I did, and at the end of our meeting he asked me how much time in his busy schedule he should devote to ethics. I told him all his time; ethics never ends, just as communications and politeness and integrity never end. He looked at me as if I was crazy. Amazingly, this unenlightened executive soon after accepted an offer as CEO of a much larger company, probably at a much larger compensation package. What a shame that he is now in a position to spread his management style to a much larger audience. I wonder if he holds an ethics meeting on Monday afternoon and then forgets about it for the remainder of the week.

Pete: One of our favorite tests of ethical behavior is being able to look yourself in the mirror and liking what you see. I think that we can, but I wonder about a few of my former friends who have lied to and cheated others. For example, I wrote a short press release for a small company and sent a bill for a few hundred dollars. When I wasn't paid a few months later and my client didn't return phone calls, I sued in small claims court. While waiting for the hearing, my client approached me and admitted that he owed me the money and wrote a check. It bounced. A month or so later I ran into him at a restaurant where he was obviously making a pitch for new business. I walked to his table, and in a loud voice told him that his check bounced. He then pulled me aside and threatened to sue me for public defamation and wrote a check that cleared. I'm pleased to say that I never saw him again.

Bill: I'm often awed by individuals who instinctively do the right thing, and wonder how they got that way. Were they born ethically mature, or did they become ethically mature as they aged? Does maturity develop in stages? Do we first become morally aware, then develop the ability to make moral decisions? Is this the old nature vs. nurture enigma?

I speak to early teens and pose ethical questions to them. For example, you're taking your brother, who turned five years old yesterday, to an amusement park. Your parents know that the price of admission is $25 for each person over five, and gives you $50.

When you arrive at the park, you learn that children under five are admitted free. When asked, about half of my audience would lie and say that their brother is under five and pocket the $25. They excuse their behavior with the old standbys: everybody does it, the big company that owns and operates the park doesn't need the money, and I need the money more than they do. Others would say that they are uncomfortable with lying, which I feel is their conscience talking to them. Their--and our-- challenge is to listen to it as the teacher of moral awareness.

I asked this same group what they would do if they purchased a pen for $2, gave the clerk at the cash register $10, and was handed change for $20. Some say 'this is my lucky day' and keep the $10 windfall, most would return it, and others are uncomfortably confused, at which point I bring up ramifications. Would you keep the $10 if you knew that the clerk was a single mother struggling to meet expenses and the store's policy is to subtract any shortfall in the cash register from her salary? My group then starts to sympathize with the clerk, and those who would keep the money or were uncomfortably confused decide to return the money. Knowing the bigger picture helped them to make the right decision.

I enjoy reading newspaper stories regarding random acts of kindness. I become more hopeful and happy to read of individuals who return wallets to rightful owners without removing either money or credit cards, others who pay for another's meal in a restaurant, give directions to lost drivers, help to fix a flat tire, donate to charities, and otherwise go out of their way to help others through a sense of duty. Such acts temper my belief that many people will seize the opportunity for unjust enrichment.

CHAPTER 21: CONFESSIONS OF TWO ETHICS JUNKIES:

THE AUTHORS ADMIT TO THEIR ADDICTION

My personal criteria for an ethical life are to not hurt anyone physically, fiscally, or emotionally. I know that they are simplistic and incomplete, but they're a start and they work for me. I know also that I have never hurt anyone physically; I am constitutionally unable to do that. I also know that I have never hurt anyone fiscally; in fact, I am well into the bonus points since I have helped many people to survive fiscal emergencies, and I am fortunate to have been able to do so. I am equally certain that I have hurt people emotionally, starting with an ex-wife who I'd guess blames me for our divorce, and a client who I couldn't invite to my daughter's wedding because he was an abusive drunk and I couldn't risk a boisterous scene. I still feel guilty about that.

On the other hand, I am comforted to know that I have clearly met two of three of my ethics criteria, and the third most of the time, so I'm batting in the .750 range which, as the saying goes, ain't all bad.

My three criteria are, of course, negative in the sense that they describe what not to do. I can make them positive and, I think— see if you agree—enter into a higher plane of human behavior.

Suppose, for example, that I help people physically; I can with simple acts of kindness such as helping an elderly neighbor to cross a busy street ... or I drive her to her doctor's...both of which I do regularly.

Suppose, again, for example, I help people fiscally, which I have done often. For example, I loaned a friend the down payment for a house because he was in a temporary bind, and another friend the seed capital for a new business venture.

I have helped people emotionally as well: I have guided and supported one friend through a contentious divorce, another through a traumatic hunt for a job. None of this is at all unusual, or is it?

As I write this, I am disturbed by the question: What if I had done nothing? Is not acting, acting?

There's a prayer for forgiveness that contains the phrase '...for things done and things left undone.' Somehow that phrase seems to make what you didn't do sound even more heinous than all those bad things that you did do!

We are all aware of what our normal duties are as a member of society: getting up and going to work, taking care of ourselves and our families, and generally doing our share, so to speak.

These duties are sort of givens — things we understand to be simply part of our responsibilities in life. And so we do them almost automatically, without much thought, because to not do them generally causes immediate and unacceptable consequences, like losing your job or precipitating divorce proceedings!

But what about those occasional situations when we are faced with a choice of either taking action or ignoring the situation? What about when we witness an act of injustice being committed? When we see one of our fellow human beings in some sort of difficulty? How about then? Do we take some action or do we walk on by, making it one of those things left undone?

The decision to take — or not to take — voluntary action and get involved when opportunities present themselves is actually a big part of our moral and ethical lives. Those decisions that we make, both by commission or omission, often affect how situations are resolved.

Be it one way or the other — getting involved or walking away — we bear a certain responsibility for a situation's outcome. There's even a reality-type TV show about these kinds of involvement decisions: 'What Would You Do?' If you've seen that show and happen to find it difficult to watch, you are not alone. Difficult situations often require courageous actions, putting yourself in a certain amount of danger.

Rushworth Kidder, founder of the Institute for Global Ethics, wrote an entire book about situations where people are called upon to make choices that involve personal sacrifice. He called it Moral Courage.

True, many such confrontational situations are not that vital. Petty arguments and seemingly inflammatory situations often cool down on their own. Occasionally, however, a critical situation may arise where your personal involvement might make an important difference in the outcome. In such a case, getting involved can be a morally courageous and ethically positive decision — and sometimes it might even end up being a matter of life or death as well. Obviously there are professions for which life-or-death decisions are, if not commonplace, at least a recognized part of the job: police and firemen, military personnel, healthcare professionals, and even engineers, upon whose handiworks we daily risk our lives. But what about the rest of us? How important is it for us to 'decide to take action'? To get involved? And why, sometimes, are we afraid to do so?

For those who prefer to avoid getting involved at all costs, here's a laundry list of excuses:

I don't have time

It's too much trouble

I really don't understand the situation

It's too dangerous and I might get hurt

It's none of my business; it's not my problem; someone
        else will take care of it

I'm too embarrassed

It might cost me money

It doesn't matter one way or the other

I'm leaving it to the cops

(If you have a personal favorite that's not on this list, please feel free to add it.)

We've all heard all of the excuses. We may even have used one or two ourselves.

You've no doubt heard the expression, 'Not to decide is to decide.' A paraphrase similarly holds true in the sort of confrontational situations we've been talking about: "Not to act is to act." And it's not true that, if you just keep on walking and don't look back, no one will know and you'll be out of there. It's not true because you will know.

- Pete Geissler

***

As head of the Beard Institute of Ethics, Sustainability, and Responsible Financial Management, a part of the Palumbo Donahue School of Business at Duquesne University from 2011-2014, a Fellow at the Wheatley Institute at Brigham Young University, a regular lecturer at the Marriott School, and an invited lecturer at the Universities of Pittsburgh, Notre Dame, Carnegie Mellon, Northwestern, Nebraska, Illinois, and Benedictine you can be sure that I am a champion of ethics as an integral part of the institution of business, all organizations, and of life itself. I am convinced that ethics should and can be habituated in the psyche and personality of every person at every level in every organization.

Like my co-author, I have my own concept of an ethical person, in business and elsewhere, and, also like my co-author, I hope that I walk the talk. My concept is lengthier and perhaps more complex: Ethical persons are truthful, respectful, trusted, and principled. They exhibit a strong sense of self awareness, acute sensitivity and a true appreciation of life and its higher meanings. They are aware of the world around them and contribute positively to fill that world with hope, love, compassion, kindness, and wisdom, and to eliminate despair, hate, self-aggrandizement, cruelty, and ignorance.

Ethical people have a predisposed inclination to treat others, all others, and nature with dignity and respect.

I arrived at this concept at a sub-conscience level while a young child, as I mentioned in CHAPTER 5 I was blessed with admirable coaches, scout leaders, teachers, priests, and parents who were instinctively dedicated to ethical behavior.

My ethical education continued during my years of working with Alcoa and its CEO, Paul O'Neill, my model for an ethical person and truly an enlightened leader. Paul intuitively obeys the habits put forth in CHAPTER 4; for example, I've never known him to willingly and capriciously interpret the rules in ways that are unfair, and I've never known him to treat others with anything but the deepest respect. He set the tone for the entire company; he expected all employees to 'do what's right at all times'; no exceptions. He challenged everyone to be and do their best and gave them the necessary tools and training to get it done.

I do not think that by any stretch of my imagination or intellect that Alcoa's impressive growth of revenues and profits, and of its reputation for quality products and as a fine, safe place to work, was coincidental or accidental. It was the result of a culture built and constantly reinforced by Paul O'Neill.

This book is riddled with my experiences at Alcoa, but they are applicable to every organization of any type. I hope that you resonate and learn from them.

- Bill O'Rourke

APPENDIX A: QUOTES, QUIPS AND INSIGHTS ABOUT ETHICS AND MORALITY:

SOME HUMOROUS, SOME HUMORLESS, ALL PERTINENT

'What is moral is what you feel good after.' Ernest Hemingway (Reminds us of the 1960s, when one rallying cry of hippies and others was if it feels good, it must be good, like free love and open marriage, both failures.)

'There is perhaps no phenomenon which contains so much destructive feeling as moral indignation, which permits envy and hate to be acted out under the guise of virtue.' Erich Fromm (We know so many self-righteous people we could write another book, but won't; you know them too.)

'Morality is the custom of one's country and the current feeling of one's peers. Cannibalism is moral in a cannibal country.' Samuel Butler. (And throwing Christians to the lions and watching gladiators kill each other was moral in ancient Rome.) Shakespeare's Hamlet agrees: *There is nothing either good or bad that thinking makes it so.* (Unfortunately true; we as a society create meanings for words, including ethics.)

'A man is ethical only when life, as such, is sacred to him, that of plants and animals as well as that of his fellow man, and when he devotes himself helpfully to all life in the need of help.' Albert Schweitzer (We agree wholeheartedly.)

'Two things fill the mind with ever new and increasing wonder— the starry heavens above me, and the moral law within me.' Immanuel Kant (We're still trying to understand the heavens and the heavenly.)

'No morality can be founded on authority, even if the authority were divine.' A.J. Ayer (Our religious friends would disagree vehemently; they insist that the Bible is the divine moral authority and it supersedes all civil authority.)

'When choosing between two evils, I always like to try the one I've never tried before.' Mae West (OK, she's playing her role. Mae made a very good living by being a vamp, or pretending to be. Dean Martin and W.C. Fields made their millions in part by pretending to be drunks.)

'Only a coward or madman would give good for evil.' Euripides

'To thine own self be true.' William Shakespeare

'Nothing is at last sacred but the integrity of your own mind.' Ralph Waldo Emerson

THE GUY IN THE GLASS

Dale Winbrow (1934)

When you get what you want in your struggle for pelf,

And the world makes you king for a day.

Then go to the mirror and look at yourself,

And see what the guy has to say.

For it isn't your Father, Mother or Wife,

Whose judgment upon you must pass.

The feller whose verdict counts most in your life Is

the guy staring back from the glass.

He's the feller to please, never mind all the rest,

For he's with you clear up to the end,

And you've passed your most dangerous, difficult test If

the guy in the glass is your friend.

You may be like Jack Horner and 'chisel' a plum,

And think you're a wonderful guy.

But the man in the glass says you're only a bum If

you can't look him straight in the eye.

You can fool the whole world down the pathway of years,

And get pats on the back as you pass.

But your final reward will be heartaches and tears If

you've cheated the guy in the glass.

APPENDIX B: ETHICS AND LAW FROM AN EXPERT:

KIDDER ISN'T KIDDING

Rushworth M. Kidder is founder and president of the Institute of Global Ethics, and a fascinating and engaging writer. In his book, How Good People Make Tough Choices, he discusses law and ethics in this way:

Law and ethics are not the same. Yet it should go without saying that obedience to law, while it is usually a necessary condition for ethical action, is not sufficient to guarantee it. Individuals who merely obey the letter of the law may or may not be ethical. That point is nicely made whenever the Ethics Committee of the United States Senate determines that because one of its members has broken no regulation, he or she is considered ethical. The wide-spread cynicism over some of the committee's determinations suggests that public faith in that misnamed body, which appears to have no interest in "ethics"... but only in laws or regulations that may have been violated. Obeying the law, then, is not enough to earn the "ethical" label.

Mr. Kidder continues on this theme in another part of his book:

...the old adage, if it ain't illegal, it must be ethical, is so deeply flawed. Ethics and law ... are as different as the unenforceable

from the enforceable. To be sure, law is a kind of condensation of
ethics into codification: it reflects areas of moral agreement so
broad that the society comes together and says, "This ethical
behavior shall be mandated."...When ethics collapses, the law
rushes in to fill the void. Why? Because regulation is essential to
sustain any kind of human experience involving two or more
people. The choice is not, "Will society be regulated?" The choice
is only between unenforceable self-regulation and enforceable
regulation...Surely a powerful indicator of ethical decay is the glut
of new laws—and new lawyers—spilling into the market each year.
If ... our ethical decay is severe, the age of hyper-regulation
cannot be far behind.

Hyper regulation scares businesspersons because their power, and
their incomes, would decrease. On the other hand, it energizes
most, maybe every, government bureaucrat because their power
and incomes would increase. In short, the balance of power would
shift to government, which is initially called socialism, and
eventually communism. Businesspersons deplore the very idea, yet
they behave as if they love it.

I'm reminded here of Norman Cousins' words: "Government in
the U.S. today is a senior partner in every business in the country."
And I'm reminded of Winston Churchill's words: "The inherent
vice of capitalism is the unequal sharing of blessings; the inherent

virtue of socialism is the equal sharing of miseries."

APPENDIX C: THE GREAT PHILOSOPHERS SPEAK ABOUT ETHICS.

THEY SHOWED US THE WAY

The authors are humbled by the many great thinkers, past and present, who have discussed ethics with insights that we can only admire and wish we could emulate. Philosophers in our universities, for example, continue to debate the issue and publish their thoughts in books and journals. Nevertheless, we feel confident enough to offer a very cursory overview; its sole intent is to pique the curiosities of readers who crave more on the subject. We also direct readers to APPENDIX G: FURTHER READING.

The great philosophers for centuries have tried to define ethical/un-ethical, and have used 'good', 'right' and' virtue' to mean ethical, and 'evil', 'wrong' and 'vice' to mean unethical.

For Plato, the good, i.e. ethical, is not a matter of opinion, but an object of knowledge. Knowledge of good and evil (unethical) is the best fruit of the tree of knowledge. Socrates agrees: 'to seek and follow one thing only … to learn and discern between good and evil.'

Aristotle does not think that ethics, or any science that deals with good and evil, can be as precise as mathematics: 'Our discussion will be adequate if it has as much clearness as the subject matter admits of, for precision is not to be sought for alike in all discussions.' Therefore, the moral sciences, such as ethics and politics, can have objective and universal validity no less than physics or mathematics, at least on the level of principles.'

Locke and Kant also affirm the scientific character of ethics, but without the qualifications that Aristotle insists upon. Locke says: 'The precise real essence of things moral words stand for may be perfectly known, and so the congruity and incongruity of the things themselves may be discovered...' Kant says the two major parts of philosophy—physics and ethics—are equal, the one concerned with the laws of nature, the other with the laws of freedom. Each is supported by empirical (derived from experience) and a priori (derived from logic) knowledge.

Spinoza writes that good and evil 'indicate nothing positive in things considered among themselves, nor are they anything else that modes of thought.' He continues: 'good is that which we certainly know is useful to us'.

Mill seems to agree with Spinoza: He offers the standards of utility as an objective principle of morality. He adds: 'The ultimate sanction of all morality is a subjective feeling in our minds...'

APPENDIX D: MORE ON THE DESTRUCTIVE ROLE OF ARROGANCE, THE CONSTRUCTIVE ROLE OF HUMILITY:

ESCHEW ONE, EMBRACE THE OTHER

One sure way to destroy lives, businesses, entire economies and nations, and, in the extreme, the entire world is to be absolutely certain that you can't.

Arrogant people typically make unilateral decisions that they are absolutely certain are correct and beneficial largely for themselves and, at times, for others, yet those same decisions often create the opposite effects. But they don't care: They are so drunk with their egomania, entitlements, power, and influence that negative consequences never enter their minds; either the consequences will never be discovered or the perpetrators delude themselves into thinking that they are above reproach or punishment of any kind.

Arrogant people and their destructions are endemic, and they share similar obnoxious traits. They're unaware of the limits of their knowledge; they are insensitive to surrounding circumstances and their own, and others', biases and points of view; are pretentious and boastful and show it by pretending to know more than they do; and lack the logic needed to support their beliefs or decisions.

In short, they are so egocentric, so wrapped up in themselves that they easily, willingly, and foolishly believe that they are omniscient and protected from errors in any part of their current and future lives. They do not consider the consequences of their decisions and actions simply because they are absolutely certain that they are 'right' for themselves and, therefore, for everyone (their intellectual and moral inferiors) who may be affected. They know what is best for others and impose that biased 'knowledge' on anyone willing to accept it.

Egocentrism is the root. Those afflicted with it judge the world from a narrow, self-serving perspective and typically are masters at self-deception and rationalization, maintain beliefs that are contrary to solid evidence, and violate ethical and moral standards while being perfectly confident of their righteousness.

A prominent and recent example in business is Jeffrey Skilling, the former VP of that icon of abject failure, ENRON. He was so certain that he was more intelligent than anyone that he belittled suggestions from associates, including those who warned that the illegal Ponzi scheme in which the company was engaged would eventually collapse, along with the entire company, needlessly destroying or upsetting countless lives.

Self-appointed seers display amazing arrogance when they

announce their predictions with certainty, but are silent when their predictions prove to be off the mark. A few examples from business: 'there is no reason anyone would want a computer in their home', said Ken Olson, top exec at Digital Equipment Corp., an icon that soon disappeared. And I was told that Blockbuster, Borders, and Blackberry faded for a similar managerial mindset. I witnessed arrogance several times in my career as a writer for businesses, and each time I was struck speechless, a painful admission for a writer. I was working with a marketing manager at a huge steel company to publicize a new, totally unrelated business: lending money to others to lease equipment and buildings. When I asked why anybody would want to borrow from the company, thinking naively that the answer might be lower interest rates or a willingness to take greater risks, I was told: 'We're xxx Steel company, and that should be enough.' I wrote a few meaningless buzz words, and was told that I was brilliant. The leasing business soon folded, and, perhaps not surprisingly given this arrogant mindset, the company is losing money and, some say, is headed for bankruptcy Let's hope that a new leader will bring enlightenment and humility.

I was working with a product development manager at Westinghouse in a similar situation, trying to figure out how to market a system to automate hospitals, a business far from the company's core expertise and strengths: the generation and use of electricity. While digging into why this particular system was better than competitors', or even trying to determine if the system had a market, I was told: 'It's from Westinghouse, and we can create and manage any business better than anyone.' Many of the anecdotes in PART II of this book demonstrate this peculiar brand of arrogance, and how it destroyed lives and companies.

Examples in the military are endemic: 'Four or five frigates will do the business without any military force', announced prime minister Lord North on dealing with the rebellious American colonies. Napoleon, feeling invincible after a series of victories, could not resist invading Russia, igniting one of the biggest and bloodiest routs and retreats in history. Hitler made the same mistake and found his Waterloo at the siege of Stalingrad and the subsequent retreat; so much for ruling the world and ridding it—in perhaps the most blatant and destructive display of arrogance and unethical behavior in history-- of undesirable, by his definition, ethnic groups.

Tojo, Japan's Prime Minister in the 1930s and 40s, overruled the wise council of Admiral Yomomoto and knew for sure that he could destroy America with his surprise attack on Pearl Harbor, but instead unleashed the greatest economic and military force ever created and he and the citizens of Japan paid dearly. How's that for ignoring the consequences of decisions? And G.W. Bush knew for sure that shock and awe would defeat the Iraqis and they would welcome democracy with open arms. His blatant display of arrogance while declaring that the worst of the fighting was over on the deck of a carrier will forever stand as an enduring icon of self-delusion.

Robert McNamara didn't play favorites; he applied the arrogance he cultivated at Harvard and Ford Motor to the Federal Government and the military. His elaborate plans, dubbed 'systems analysis', for waging the Viet Nam war were spectacular failures with one exception: they convinced the military that being flexible, able to adjust with changing conditions, was more successful than staying the course at any cost.

Perhaps the best examples are in government at every level and persuasion, but particularly the bureaucrats who are totally convinced that they know how to spend your money and live your life better than you do. Examples abound and their destruction runs the gamut from local and picky to global and monumental. On the local and picky side is the council of a small town near Pittsburgh that wants to ban outdoor grilling within five feet of a home, citing the need to prevent fires while admitting that none from this obscure source has ever been reported. Mayor Bloomberg of New York City has decided that you cannot buy a soda that tips the scales at over 16 ounces, arguing that he is protecting your health. How does he know? On a national scale, President Obama has decided that you will fill your gas tank with more and more ethanol and spend your money to subsidize electric cars, citing the goal of energy independence despite the obvious life-cycle truth that producing ethanol and running battery-powered cars use more oil than they save.

Bill Clinton fits the pattern: I feel certain that he never once thought that his dalliances with Monica in the Oval Office would be revealed and cause his impeachment trial by his many vindictive enemies. Could that one arrogant error prevent him from being lauded by historians as one of our best presidents?

In sports, Tiger Woods surely did not expect to be caught cheating on his wife, and when he was he lost many millions of dollars and the respect of millions of fans. Ben Roethlisberger, the Steelers' quarterback, followed the same path but, he says, is now a reformed family man. Pete Rose was caught gambling on the team he was playing against, apparently not realizing the conflict of interest or, if he did, being convinced that his all-but-assured all-star status would shield him from any consequences. He was wrong.

Arrogance is akin to pride—the seventh deadly sin and the root and composite of all sins-- with at least one possible exception: Recent research suggests that our brains are programmed for pride, and there isn't anything we can do to prevent it. Perhaps we are more in control of our arrogance, perhaps not. Pride is also good in the sense that we should all be proud of our positive accomplishments. Pride is bad when we think of ourselves as better than others, a form of arrogance.

THE FOUR RELATED TRAITS OF ARROGANT PEOPLE: AVOID THEM

1. Secrecy : arrogant people hide their thoughts and actions, probably because down deep they know that they are wrong.
2. Unwillingness or inability to listen to advice from others who often know more about the situation, or to just listen, quietly, to learn.
3. Unwillingness or inability to visualize or project the future consequences of current decisions. We've come back to this thought several time in this book simply because it is so endemic. Log on to 'wrong predictions' and read Useless Arithmetic by Orrin Pinkey and you'll see what we mean.
4. Greed, accompanied by fallacious attempts to justify excessive

salaries and bonuses and other forms of compensation as if they are entitled to them.

HOW ARROGANCE HELPED DESTROY A HOUSEHOLD NAME

When arrogance runs amok, whole companies can crash and burn. Westinghouse is one example. Its CEOs were enamored at various times with the following strategic directions, all of which proved to be wrong and destructive:

1. We can be successful in any business' (the drive to be the world's most diversified company by entering unrelated business such as bottled water, hospital automation, watches, vacation properties, low-income housing)
2. I'm absolutely certain that the price of uranium will rise' (speculation , aka greed and certainty, blindness to reality)
3. My private life is private, and I refuse to change' (how an alleged affair destroyed morale and productivity)
4. Real estate and second mortgages pay big and we know how to play the game'(the impetus of managing for stockholder value, the crash of Westinghouse Credit and how/why a buyout was refused)

HUMILITY: IDENTIFYING THE AMAZING, SAVING GRACE

One way to enhance lives, businesses, entire economies and countries, and to bring peace and harmony to the world …
…is to be so humble that you try.

Humble persons demonstrate awareness of the need to face and fairly address ideas, beliefs, or viewpoints toward which they are strongly opposed and/or have not seriously considered. They also demonstrate empathy toward and understanding of others by putting aside their own egocentricity. They avoid selective memory by thoughtfully considering and accepting, when appropriate, evidence from others that does not support their beliefs and decisions. They avoid oversimplification of complex issues and instead drill down by asking the why and how questions that discover a greater understanding of truth and morality. In short, they live with open minds and communicate openly and honestly.

Pope Francis fits that mold as well as anyone. He was recognized by Time Magazine as the 2013 Man of the Year by demonstrating humility to the world. Ronald Reagan fits that mold as well. No doubt his ego was huge, having risen from a lower-echelon actor to President. But he was humble in that he knew the limits of his intelligence and energies: he surrounded himself with competent advisers and listened to them before making crucial decisions—teamwork at its zenith. He also never wavered from his social and economic principles, igniting the most affluent era in the history of the world, benefitting his successors and billions of others.

A prominent sign of humility is interpersonal skills, or, as Daniel Goldman points out in his book, Emotional Intelligence, interpersonal intelligence: the ability to understand what motivates others and how they think and behave ... the capacity to discern and respond appropriately to moods, temperaments, motivations, and desires.

Jim Browne, in CHAPTER 18, calls interpersonal skills extremely important for success but it must be coupled with ethics. He develops powerful and sustainable empathy with his clients by co-operating with them to develop their emotional quotient, aka tolerance for risk, before he invests one dime of their money. He is far too humble to think that he knows the goals and aspirations of his clients better than they do.

Humility is demonstrated by willingness to change in constructive, sustainable ways. It has been defined in other ways by many of the world's great thinkers, always as a prime virtue:

"Humility is the solid foundation of all virtues." Confucius

"The first test of a truly great man is humility." John Ruskin

"Better is to be of a humble spirit with the lowly, than to divide the spoil with the proud." Proverbs 16:10

"Meekness (humility) is nothing more than a true knowledge of oneself as one is. Anyone who truly knows himself will be meek (humble) indeed." The Cloud of Unknowing

"A humble person lives on earth as if in the Kingdom of heaven - always happy, peaceful and satisfied with everything."
St. Anthony of Optina

"True humility is not thinking less of yourself; it is thinking of yourself less." C.S. Lewis, Mere Christianity

"There is nothing noble in being superior to your fellow man; true nobility is being superior to your former self." Ernest Hemingway

"It was pride that changed angels into devils; it is humility that makes men as angels." Saint Augustine

"Humility is like underwear: essential, but indecent if it shows." Helen Nielson

"Humility and knowledge in poor clothes excel pride and ignorance in costly attire." William Penn

APPENDIX E: THE LAW OF UNINTENDED CONSEQUENCES:

IT REARS ITS UGLY AND PRETTY HEAD WHEN LEAST EXPECTED

Sociologist Robert K. Merton popularized the law of unintended consequences (The Law, hereafter) in his 1936 paper, *The Unanticipated Consequences of Purposive Social Action*. In it, Merton attempted to systematically analyze the problem of unintended consequences of deliberate acts intended to cause social change. More recently, The Law has come to be a warning that intervention in a complex situation tends to create unanticipated consequences that can be:

• Positive, an unexpected benefit usually attributed to good fortune or luck (which can be tricky since there is some truth in the aphorisms that luck favors the wise and the prepared).
• Negative, an unexpected detriment in addition to the positive benefit, usually attributed to bad luck or fortune; and/or
• Perverse, contrary to the original intent; when the intended consequence worsens the outcome, usually attributed to stupidity or ignorance. Violations of the law are perpetrated by arrogance, as is unethical behavior. In both cases, the perpetrators believe that they can accurately predict future consequences (nobody can), and/or they believe that any consequences will be ignored

or even accepted by others (possible, but not certain). Other causes might be ignorance based on incomplete analysis; honest error based on incorrect analysis; and short-sightedness that is typically based on immediate, egocentric interests that ignore the longer term. The impacts of The Law are evident in the anecdotes related in PART II: For example, on the side of positive consequences, when Pete Geissler refused to be intimidated by clients, he was showered with contracts from other clients in the same firm.

On the side of negative consequences, the Quality Control engineer in CHAPTER 16 surely didn't think that he would lose his job when he fudged inspection records; he did because he didn't predict or understand the importance of quality and adhering to corporate values held by his superiors.

On the perverse side, top managers never believed that a research engineer, in CHAPTER 5, would resign over an ethical issue that they, the managers, refused to recognize but Joe thought was vitally important. In essence, the managers were ignorant of Joe's passionate need to resolve the issue: the company lost a valuable employee and Joe gained his peace of mind.

An aside for interested readers, here are some famous and infamous unintended consequences. Positive: aspirin was found to have beneficial health effects beyond relieving pain; Negative: prohibition led to more bars and more drinking as citizens rebelled; and Perverse: The automobile has increased mobility but also air pollution, millions of accidental deaths and injuries, and loss of wildlife habitats.

APPENDIX F: MORE ON CONSIDERATIONS OF AUTHORITY AND TIME:

CONTROLLED EXPERIMENTS PROVE THE POINTS

Blind obedience to authority is rampant in all organizations with a hierarchal structure of control, and is perhaps more rampant during recessions when employees fear retribution in the form of losing their jobs or a promotion. In some cultures, authorities dictate behavior well beyond what we in the United States currently consider acceptable. The powerful influence of obedience to authority has also been demonstrated experimentally.

For example, the Milgram experiments of the 1960s examined the extent to which authority can dull one's ethical sensibilities. Milgram recruited volunteers who were told they would be participating in a study designed to improve learning. The volunteers, supervised by a researcher wearing that universal symbol of authority, a white lab coat, were instructed to administer electrical shocks each time the "learner" – an actor who was not actually being shocked, on the other side of a partition made an error in the learning exercise.

As the experiment progressed and the actor-learner continued to make mistakes, the volunteers administering the exercise were told to increase the voltage, even as the actor-learner began to scream, bang on the walls, and plead for the experiment to end. Beginning at 15 volts, all twenty-six volunteers progressed to 300 volts, and twelve volunteers continued, under the direction of the authority figure, to administer shocks to the ultimate 450 volt level, which was clearly labeled on the machine as 'danger, severe shock.' When asked to justify their actions, research participants most commonly explain that they were just doing what they were told to do.

Similar subsequent studies have confirmed Milgram's results.

Researchers studying the pressures of time told seminary students that they were enrolling in a research study about religious education, then directed the seminarians to walk a prescribed path to a nearby building where they would deliver an impromptu sermon on the parable of the Good Samaritan. All seminarians took the same path to the nearby building, along which they encountered an actor who was slumped in a doorway, pretending to be in obvious distress. The only variable was the sense of urgency relayed to the seminarians. One-third were given the 'high hurry' message that they were already late to deliver their sermon, one-third were given a less urgent 'intermediate hurry' message, and the final third was told they had plenty of time, but that they should go ahead and proceed to the preaching venue.

The seminarians were on their way to deliver a talk on the virtues of stopping to assist someone in need of help, and yet only 63% of those given the low hurry message, 45% of those given the intermediate hurry message, and 10% of those given the "high hurry" message stopped to offer their help to the actor planted along the route. Having to literally step over the individual needing help, many seminarians arrived to deliver their Good Samaritan sermon with noticeable distress caused by their conflict between the good of arriving on time and performing a requested task pursuant to the expectations of others and the good of helping a stranger in need (consistent with the sermon that must have been running through their minds). Others, however, blinded by the time pressures and a focus on the task at hand were not even aware of the ethical dilemma in their midst.

APPENDIX G: FURTHER READING:

WITH COMMENTS FROM THE AUTHORS

Business Ethics: A Field Guide, by Bradley Agle, Aaron Miller, and Bill O'Rourke, to be published in Fall 2014. (See Appendix H for more.)

Emotional Intelligence: Why it can matter more than IQ, by Daniel Goleman, Bantam Books, 1995, 350 pages. The Harvard Business Review hailed this book as a ground-breaking, paradigm-shifting idea, one of the most influential business books of the decade. We think of it as a close relative to ethical maturity, and we highly suggest reading it as a an adjunct to this book.

Defining Moments: When Managers must Choose between Right and Right, by Joseph L. Badaracco, Jr. Harvard Business Press, 1997, 147 pages.

The Elements of Ethics for Professionals, by W. Brad Johnson and Charles R. Ridley. Palgrave MacMillan, 2008, 213 pages.

The Ethical Executive: Becoming Aware of the Root Causes of Unethical Behavior--45 Psychological Traps that Every One of us Falls Prey to, by Robert Hoyk and Paul Hersey. Stanford Business Books. 213 pages.

Giving Voice to Values: How to Speak your Mind When you Know What's Right, by Mary C. Gentile. Yale University Press, 2010, 320 pages. Mary Gentile stresses the importance of an organizational culture that allows and encourages employees to speak up on ethical issues and assures that employees are heard when they have the courage to speak. The fact that over 400 organizations have adopted the "Giving Voice to Values" program vouches for its value.

How Good People Make Tough Choices: Resolving the Dilemma-mas of Ethical Living, by Rushworth M. Kidder. Harper, 1995, updated and released in 2009. 255 pages. This fast-paced, insightful, enthralling book had such a positive influence on my thinking about ethics and how I can behave more ethically that I gave copies to a half-dozen friends and started a discussion group. Concepts are supported vividly by case studies to which I can resonate.

How Will You Measure Your Life, by Clayton Christensen, James

Allworth & Karen Dillon, HarperCollins publishers (2012). In this book, the authors ask readers how to be happy in their career and in their relationships, and to stay out of jail. They urge us to pause and think before acting, and offer useful suggestions on how to think about life in general. They suggest that there are many theories and models from which we can learn and apply to our lives to assure they will be 'successful' and 'happy.' By thinking about measuring our life the ethical dimensions of our journey become so apparent - helping others; being kind, honest and forgiving; and committing to our careers and relationships. I believe that this book is a vivid demonstration of how powerful ethics (including honesty, justice, fairness, etc.) is in our lives.

Managing Business Ethics: Straight Talk about How to do it Right (5th edition), by Linda Trevino and Katherine Nelson. John Wiley & Sons, 2011, 460 pages. This book is used in many ethics courses in business schools. It is a thorough, pragmatic presentation of the complex ethical issues that we all face in our lives and provides sound recommendations for choosing ethical behavior. I believe that Linda Trevino and Katherine Nelson have made the world a better place through their book.

The Power of Habit by Charles Duhigg. Charles Duhigg explains human inertia and the difficulty of changing our habits, and urges us to build 'good' habits and modify existing, destructive patterns to better our lives. He tells us and shows us through real life examples that a life of habitual excellence is achievable, and challenges us to transform our businesses, our communities, and our lives.

Virtuous Leadership: An Agenda for Personal Excellence, by Alexandre Havard. Scepter Press, 2007. A must-read for anyone who understands or who wants to understand more deeply the symbiotic dependencies of leadership and ethics. The book is resonating with leaders in government, business, and religion.

APPENDIX H: THE THIRTEEN MOST COMMON BUSINESS ETHICSDILEMMAS,

AND WHERE THEY ARE ADDRESSED IN THIS BOOK

Do inquiring minds focused on the same topic draw similar conclusions? And, if they do, is the credibility and validity of those conclusions enhanced? The authors (one of whom, in the interests of ethical full disclosure, is Bill O'Rourke) of Business Ethics: A Field Guide, have identified and formally listed thirteen ethical dilemmas most often faced by people in business (and, we feel, in other parts of life as well).

They then expanded the discussion by posing questions to ask before analyzing and resolving the dilemmas. The Power of Ethics addresses the same and other dilemmas less formally, largely in the anecdotes of Part II, Chapters 5 through nineteen, and Appendices B and F. The books were written independently and at different times.

THE THIRTEEN DILEMMAS

ABOUT THE AUTHORS

Pete Geissler is a professional writer of business and technical knowledge, and a former adjunct professor of Advanced Professional and Technical Writing at Carnegie Mellon University and Senior Lecturer in Writing at The Graduate School of Environmental Science and Management, Duquesne University. Other books he has authored include The Power of Being Articulate, The Power of Writing Well, The Power of Dignity, and Divorce can be Such Sweet Sorrow.

For more: www.TheExpressivePress.com.
Email: geissler@earthlink.net
Linkedin: https://www.linkedin.com/pub/pete-geissler/20/783/b52

Bill O'Rourke culminated his long career at Alcoa as the Vice President of Environment, Health & Safety and Sustainability reporting to the CEO. In addition to his three-year assignment as President of Alcoa-Russia, Bill held increasingly responsible positions in law, environmental affairs, health & safety, procurement, information technology, auditing, and global business services. He was the Executive Director of the Beard Institute (which focuses on ethics, sustainability and responsible financial management), a part of the Palumbo-Donahue School of Business at Duquesne University. He now sits on the Board of Directors of Alcoa Foundation and Sustainable Pittsburgh, and is a Fellow in Ethics at the Wheatley Institution at Brigham Young University. Bill lectures and hosts workshops on ethics and leadership at a number of universities and other organizations throughout North America.

www.ingramcontent.com/pod-product-compliance
Lightning Source LLC
Chambersburg PA
CBHW051908170526
45168CB00001B/292

* 9 781511 834353 *